modern indian cooking

hari nayak and vikas khanna

Published by Echo Point Books & Media
Brattleboro, Vermont
www.EchoPointBooks.com

Modern Indian Cooking
ISBN: 978-1-63561-735-1 (casebound)

Creative direction by Prajakta Karandikar
Art direction by Prajakta Karandikare
Interior design by PrajaDesign Inc., www.prajadesign.com

Cover design by Adrienne Núñez

Cover images: *FC top:* Indian dish of scallops, by jackjayDigital, LLC, © Jack
Turkel; *FC bottom:* set of aromatic Indian spices and condiments , by MLunov,
courtesy of CreativeMarket

Author photographs by Ken Jones

modern indian cooking

"the next generation of indian cooking"

EPBM

ECHO POINT BOOKS & MEDIA, LLC
Brattleboro, Vermont

Contents

Foreword

The title of the book, **Modern Indian Cooking,** has many meanings for food lovers.

Not so long ago, the use of spices and the word curry had a different perception which changed as it traveled towards the west.

Like every other cuisine, Indian cooking is always evolving and accepting new flavors from globalization and also inspiring chefs all over the world to use Indian ingredients in their cuisine.

Whether cooking for large groups of guests or cooking for family, home cooks share a common thread with a professional chef that is the care and love they take in preparing the food. This is the main ingredient used in **Modern Indian Cooking.**

Vikas Khanna and Hari Nayak have been adding the flavor of India in so many ways to our kitchens and lives. Their passion for the culinary arts and the drive to reach out to the communities around the world, have given new dimensions to food.

With this book they bring together traditional Indian flavors with fresh modern interpretations!

Congratulations Vikas and Hari for creating **Modern Indian Cooking.**

Daniel Boulud

Introduction

This book represents our take on modern Indian cuisine whether cooked for the family or for guests, prepared using fresh ingredients, or designed to accommodate the modern lifestyle. Indian cooking is often perceived as intimidating due to the use of a wide range of unusual ingredients and complex cooking procedures. Our book is an attempt to recreate classic Indian dishes by using simplistic techniques along with a delicious juxtaposition of non-Indian ingredients. We have strived to bring traditional Indian cuisine to simplified levels fit for modern living and entertaining, while keeping the flavors and authenticity intact.

Modern Indian Cooking celebrates the grandeur of the food of India while preserving the character of each region's distinctive style of cooking. While creating this book we have taken into account the different ways we cook and eat food in modern life and the new kinds of ingredients that are now readily available. This book adapts a contemporary style of cooking great tasting food for easy entertaining or a busy lifestyle. It provides a wonderful insight into the richly diverse nation of India and the many flavors it brings to our tables.

black cardamom

chili powder

cloves

cardamom

curry leaves

cumin

sage

ginger

saffron

star anise

Seasonings

Spices, we cannot imagine a world without spices. The first fragmented but authentic records of the use of herbs and spices date from the Pyramid Age in Egypt, around 2600 to 2100 BC. Onions and garlic were fed to 100,000 laborers who toiled in the construction of the great pyramids for their medicinal properties and to preserve health.

Indian cuisine arguably uses more spices than any other, a legacy of the number of spices grown in India and the long history of trading Indian spices for spices from other parts of the world. Some of the main spices and herbs used in Indian cuisine include coriander seed, turmeric, cinnamon, cumin, fenugreek, ginger, pepper, chili, nutmeg, mace, cloves, tamarind, cardamom and saffron. However, we have incorporated global flavors from Latin America, the Far East, Europe and the Mediterranean into traditional Indian flavors to create a unique and exciting combination and spice blends.

Spices fall into five key flavor groups: sweet, pungent, tangy, hot and amalgamating. Herbs belong to a savory group and can be further classified as mild, medium, strong or pungent. The flavor grouping is a useful guide to the relative quantities of these spices that should be used when making flavor blends. When combining spices and herbs, it is important to take into consideration these characteristics.

coriander seeds

garlic

cinnamon

turmeric

fennel seeds

bay leaves

thyme

peppercorns

garam masala

red chili

mustard seeds

Curry is a blend of sweet, pungent, hot and amalgamating spices that can be mixed in literally hundreds of different proportions to make a mixture to suit particular foods. For instance, red meats will require a stronger flavored blend than seafood or vegetables. The versatility of Indian spice blends can be surprising when combined with global flavors. For example, olive oil, sage, lemon juice and curry powder make a quick, tasty vinaigrette. The addition of Indian spice blends during traditional American barbecuing or grilling gives a lot of added flavor. It is very interesting how the addition of the Mexican flavor of chilies or subtle variations of mixed herbs with Indian spice blends can create a completely different tasty dish.

Herbs, spices and ingredients that we have used in the preparation of our recipes should not be the limit in creating your unique combination; however, here are some of the non-traditional ingredients that complement Indian food: paprika, Mexican chilies (Ancho, chipotle, pasilla, mulato, guajillo) Sichuan pepper, wasabi, soy sauce, sambal paste, sage, tarragon, thyme, lemon grass and Thai basil to name a few.

"Food is our common ground, a universal experience."
—James Beard

Appetizers

Spicy Pan Seared Scallops
with Cilantro Chimmichuri

Crispy Fried Fish with
Chili Mayo

Ginger and Lemon
Grilled Chicken

Crispy Wonton Chat

Orange Chicken with
Soy Ginger Reduction

Crispy Pan Fried Shrimp
with Tamarind Glaze

Ancho Chili Paneer Kebabs with
Pomegranate Seeds

Masala Trail Mix

Mung Bean and Spinach Turnovers

Lemon Thyme Paneer Shashlik

Wasabi Chili Lamb Kebab

Flame Crisp Pappadams

Spicy Pan Seared Scallops with Cilantro Chimmichuri

Serves 6

½ pound fresh sea scallops
1 teaspoon cayenne pepper
1 teaspoon freshly ground black pepper
½ teaspoon garlic salt
3 tablespoons vegetable oil

Cilantro Chimmichuri

Makes 2 cups

1 bunch cilantro, chopped
2 tablespoons mint leaves, chopped
1 green chili, chopped
½ medium red onion, chopped
4 cloves garlic
¾ cup olive oil
Salt to taste

Rinse sea scallops and pat dry with a towel, using a sharp paring knife make criss-cross slits on top of the scallops. In a small bowl, mix together the cayenne, black pepper and garlic salt. Gently roll the scallops in the spices. Heat a nonstick skillet over medium-high heat until very hot. Pour in the oil and heat until it just begins to smoke. Carefully place each scallop in the pan flat side down.

Cook for 2 minutes per side flipping once.

In a food processor, combine cilantro, mint, chili, onion and garlic. Process until finely chopped. With machine running, pour olive oil in a steady stream through the feed tube and process until smooth. Season with salt.

Cover with plastic wrap and refrigerate until ready to use. This sauce can also be used for dipping or as marinade for seafood, poultry or meat.

Serve the scallops with the chimmichuri sauce.

Crispy Fried Fish with Chili Mayo

Serves 6

4 skinless tilapia fillets (1½ to 2 pound), cut into strips

Juice of 2 lemons

Salt to taste

½ tablespoon ground coriander

1 cup all-purpose flour

1 (4-inch) ginger, minced

3 cloves garlic, minced

1 teaspoon cumin seeds

2 tablespoons mint leaves, chopped

Salt to taste

Canola oil, for deep-frying

2 tablespoons sambal chili paste

1 tablespoon green onions, minced

2 cups low fat mayonnaise

Lemon wedges, for serving

Wash and clean the fish fillets and pat dry on paper towels. Transfer the fillets to a bowl and squeeze the lemon juice and season with salt and coriander. Marinate for an hour in the refrigerator.

Remove the fish fillets from the marinade and place on paper towels to remove any excess marinade.

In a medium bowl, combine the flour with 1½ cups water and make a smooth paste of coating consistency. Add the ginger, garlic, cumin seeds, mint leaves and salt.

Heat the oil in a wok or a deep-frying pan over medium heat to 350°F. Coat the fish fillets with the flour mixture and fry until golden brown and crisp, about 6 minutes. Remove with a slotted spoon and drain on a paper towel. Transfer to a serving dish and serve hot with lemon wedges and chili mayo dipping sauce.

To make the dipping sauce, stir the chili paste and green onions into the mayonnaise until blended.

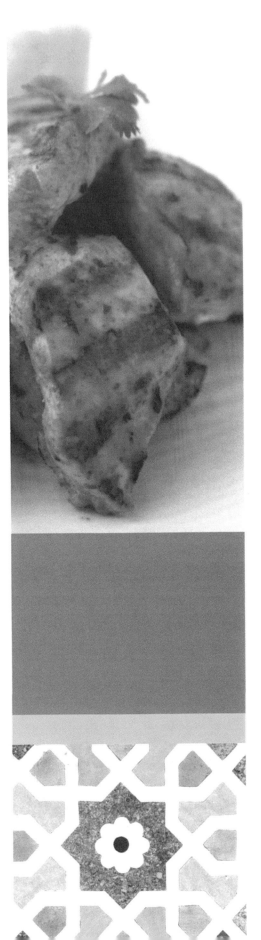

Ginger and Lemon Grilled Chicken

Serves 6

1 cup plain yogurt, whisked until smooth

1 tablespoon cumin powder

1 tablespoon garam masala

1 teaspoon chili powder

1 (4-inch) piece of fresh ginger, minced

Salt to taste

Juice of 2 lemons

8 cloves garlic, finely chopped

2 pounds boneless, skinless chicken breasts, cut into 2-inch cubes

In a large bowl, mix the yogurt, cumin powder, garam masala, chili powder, ginger, salt, lemon juice and garlic. Add the chicken and toss until coated with marinade. Cover and refrigerate for 2 to 3 hours.

Preheat grill pan or indoor electric grill to high.

Place chicken on hot grill and cook for 5 or 6 minutes on each side, until charred at edges and firm in the middle.

Serve hot.

Crispy Wonton Chat

Serves 6

1 package egg roll wrappers (4 ½ x 5 ½ inch)

Vegetable oil, for deep-frying

1 cup yogurt, whisked until smooth

Salt to taste

½ tablespoon cumin seeds, roasted and ground

1 teaspoon sugar

1 teaspoon chili powder

1 large potato, boiled, peeled and diced into
½-inch cubes

1 medium onion, finely chopped

1 (15-ounce) can chickpeas, drained and rinsed

½ cup garlic chutney (page 176)

2 tablespoons pomegranate mint chutney (page 178)

½ cup pineapple, diced

2 tablespoons cilantro, chopped

Cut the egg roll wrappers into 1-inch strips. Heat the oil in large wok and heat to 350°F over medium heat. Fry the egg roll strips until crisp and golden brown, 3 to 5 minutes. Remove with a slotted spoon and drain on paper towels.

To the whisked yogurt add salt, ground cumin, sugar and chili powder. Set aside. Mix together the potato, onion and chickpeas in a medium bowl.

On a serving plate, put half of the crispy wonton strips in the first layer. Place the potatoes, onions and chickpeas over it. Arrange remaining crisps over the potato mixture. Top with the yogurt mixture, garlic and mint chutneys, and pineapple chunks.

Serve immediately, garnished with cilantro.

Crispy Pan Fried Shrimp with Tamarind Glaze

Crispy Pan Fried Shrimp with Tamarind Glaze

Serves 6

1 pound medium-sized fresh shrimp, cleaned, shelled and deveined

1 teaspoon ginger, minced

4 teaspoons garlic, minced

1 teaspoon ground cumin

1 tablespoon tamarind paste

1 teaspoon cayenne pepper

½ teaspoon turmeric powder

1 tablespoon all-purpose flour

Salt to taste

¼ cup vegetable oil

Juice of 1 lemon

2 tablespoons Thai basil, chopped

Using a clean kitchen towel, pat dry the shrimp and set aside. Mix ginger and garlic with cumin powder. Add tamarind, cayenne pepper, turmeric, flour and salt. Stir 2 tablespoons of oil into the mixture. Transfer to a bowl, add the shrimp and toss well to coat evenly, cover and refrigerate for about 2 hours for best results.

Heat the remaining oil in a large saucepan over medium heat. Add the marinated shrimp and cook for a minute on high heat. Turn the shrimp over and cook for another minute. Reduce the heat and cook for 2 to 3 minutes, turning the shrimp occasionally for uniform cooking. Sprinkle with lemon juice and Thai basil and serve hot.

Orange Chicken with Soy Ginger Reduction

Serves 4

¼ cup soy sauce
½ cup fresh orange juice
Zest of 1 orange
4 teaspoons vegetable oil
2 tablespoons honey
1 tablespoon green chili, minced
1 teaspoon garam masala
1 (2-inch) ginger, minced
2 cloves garlic, crushed
4 skinless boneless chicken breasts, cut in half
Orange slices for garnish

In a small microwave-safe bowl, combine the soy sauce, orange juice, orange zest, oil, honey, chili, garam masala, ginger and garlic. Heat in microwave on medium for 1 minute and then stir.

Place chicken breasts in a shallow dish. Pour soy sauce mixture over the chicken and set aside to marinate for 15 to 20 minutes.

Preheat a grill to medium-high heat. Drain marinade from chicken into a small saucepan. Bring to a boil and simmer over medium heat until it reduces to half, about 5 minutes. Set aside for basting.

Lightly oil the grill. Cook chicken on the prepared grill 6 to 8 minutes per side, or until juices run clear. Baste frequently with remaining marinade until the chicken turns golden brown. Serve with orange slices and soy reduction.

Ancho Chili Paneer Kebabs with Pomegranate Seeds

Serves 6

1 cup sour cream

1 tablespoon garlic, minced

2 tablespoons ginger, minced

2 teaspoons pomegranate seeds, ground

1½ teaspoons garam masala

3 teaspoons ancho chili powder

½ teaspoon cumin seeds, roasted and ground

½ teaspoon coriander seeds, roasted and ground

Salt to taste

8 ounces paneer cheese, cut into (3-inch) pieces about ½-inch thick

Lime wedges for garnish

In a medium bowl, mix together the sour cream, garlic, ginger, pomegranate seeds, garam masala, ancho chili powder, cumin, coriander and salt.

Add to the paneer cheese, making sure that all the pieces are well coated. Cover and marinate in the refrigerator for 4 to 6 hours.

Preheat the broiler. Grease a baking tray.

Drain the marinade and transfer the paneer cheese piece by piece to the baking tray.

Broil on the top rack until golden brown, about 5 minutes on each side.

Do not over cook as paneer will toughen.

Serve hot with lemon wedges.

Masala Trail Mix

Makes 6 cups

2 teaspoons cumin seeds, dry-roasted and coarsely ground
3 teaspoons chat masala
1 teaspoon chili powder
1 teaspoon black salt
1 cup canola oil
1 cup almonds
1 cup pistachios
1 cup cashew nuts
1 cup peanuts
1 cup pumpkin or sunflower seeds
1 cup wasabi peas
1 teaspoon dried mint

Mix together the cumin seeds, chat masala, chili powder and black salt in a small bowl.

Heat the oil in a medium-sized saucepan over medium heat and fry the nuts until golden, about 1 to 2 minutes. Drain the oil as much as possible using a slotted spatula. (Do not drain them on a paper towel, or the spices will not adhere.)

Transfer nuts into a medium bowl. Quickly add the spice mixture and toss well, making sure that the nuts are well coated.

In the same pan stir-fry the seeds over medium low heat until the seeds are fragrant and golden, about 1 minute. Add the spiced nuts and toss together. Add mint and wasabi peas and adjust the seasoning to taste.

Cool completely and serve or transfer to an airtight container. This can be stored up to 3 to 4 weeks.

Mung Bean and Spinach Turnovers

Serves 6

2 tablespoons vegetable oil

1 teaspoon cumin seeds

1½ tablespoons ginger, minced

1 green chili, minced

1 tablespoon ground coriander

1¼ cups dried mung beans, washed, soaked and drained

¼ teaspoon turmeric

Salt to taste

1 cup water

1 cup chopped fresh spinach

6 phyllo pastry sheets

2 tablespoons melted butter

1 egg, whisked for glaze

Heat the oil in a large non stick saucepan over medium heat and add the cumin, ginger, green chili and coriander. Stir for about 30 seconds. Mix in the mung beans, turmeric and salt and stir about 2 minutes.

Add the water, lower the heat to medium low , cover the pan and cook until all the water has been absorbed and the mung beans are soft, about 10 to 15 minutes Add the spinach and stir until wilted, about 1 minute. Cool the mixture.

Preheat the oven to 350°F, grease a baking tray.

Brush each phyllo sheet with melted butter and stack one on top of the other. With a sharp knife, cut lengthwise into 4 equal strips, each about 3-inches wide. Stack again and cover with a damp clean kitchen towel. Cut each strip into 6 squares.

Place phyllo strips lengthwise in front of you on the work surface and spoon a generous tablespoon of the filling in the center. Brush all around the edges of each with egg glaze. Fold the right corner over the filling to the left side to make a triangle. Repeat to make more turnovers.

Place the turnovers on the baking sheet and brush with egg glaze. Bake until crisp and golden, about 20 minutes. Transfer to cooling racks.

Serve warm or at room temperature.

Lemon Thyme
Paneer Shashlik

Serves 4

1¼ cups plain yogurt

1 teaspoon ground turmeric

1 (1-inch) piece ginger, minced

4 cloves garlic, minced

2 tablespoons lemon juice

5 tablespoons lemon thyme, chopped

Salt to taste

10 ounces paneer, diced

2 green bell peppers, diced

1 medium onion, diced

2 firm tomatoes, diced

2 tablespoons vegetable oil

Mix the yogurt, turmeric, ginger, garlic, lemon juice, lemon thyme and salt in a large bowl. Add the paneer and vegetables to the marinade, cover and refrigerate for about 3 to 4 hours.

Preheat the broiler. Using eight metal skewers, thread 5 pieces of paneer pepper, onion, and tomato onto each, dividing the vegetables equally. Brush with oil. Bake for 3 to 4 minutes on each side, or until the paneer and vegetables are cooked and slightly charred around the edges. Serve hot.

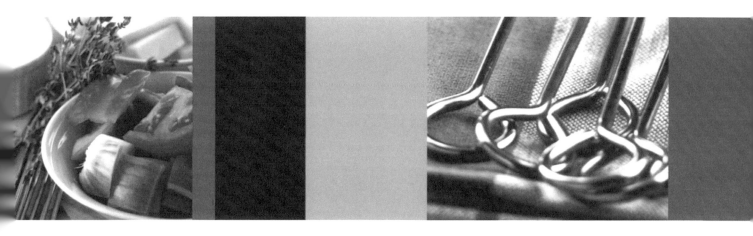

Flame Crisp Pappadams

Wasabi Chili Lamb Kebab

Serves 4

5 cloves garlic , crushed

1 (2-inch) piece ginger, chopped

3 green chilies, chopped

1 onion, chopped

3 tablespoons plain yogurt

4 tablespoons cilantro leaves

1 pound lamb, ground

Salt to taste

3 teaspoons wasabi paste

1 tablespoon Tabasco® green pepper sauce

Lemon wedges for garnish

Combine the garlic, ginger, chilies, onion, yogurt and cilantro leaves in a food processor to form a smooth paste. In a large bowl, combine the ground lamb, ground paste, salt, wasabi and green pepper sauce. Mix well. Divide the meat into 16 portions. Shape each portion into an oval patty, cover and chill for 1 hour.

Preheat the broiler to high. Using four metal skewers, thread four meatballs onto each skewer. Broil for 7 to 10 minutes until slightly brown on top. Turn over and broil the other side. Serve with lemon wedges.

Flame Crisp Pappadams

Pappadams are dried disks of dough made from legume flours. They are often flavored with chili, black pepper, garlic and cumin seeds. Some will be brittle and so thin that they're almost translucent, while others will be relatively thick and made perhaps from a different kind of legume or lentils. Pappadams are a great way to bring flavor and texture to a meal.

There are several different ways to cook pappadams. A common way is to deep-fry them, by sliding them one at a time into a skillet filled with hot oil. They will instantly start to expand and change color. With a pair of tongs, try to hold each one under the surface of the oil until the whole disk has cooked, a process that should take no more than 10 seconds. Remove from the fryer, drain excess oil and stack them to cool and become crisp. Another method to cook the pappadams is to hold each one over a flame of a gas burner or a grill, quickly exposing all sides and edges to the heat. They crinkle up into beautiful shapes almost at once and as they cool, they become very crisp. They can be formed into pockets, rolls or any desired shapes before they cool. Cooked pappadams can be stuffed or topped with toasted coconut, chopped herbs, spice mixtures, mince meats and nuts.

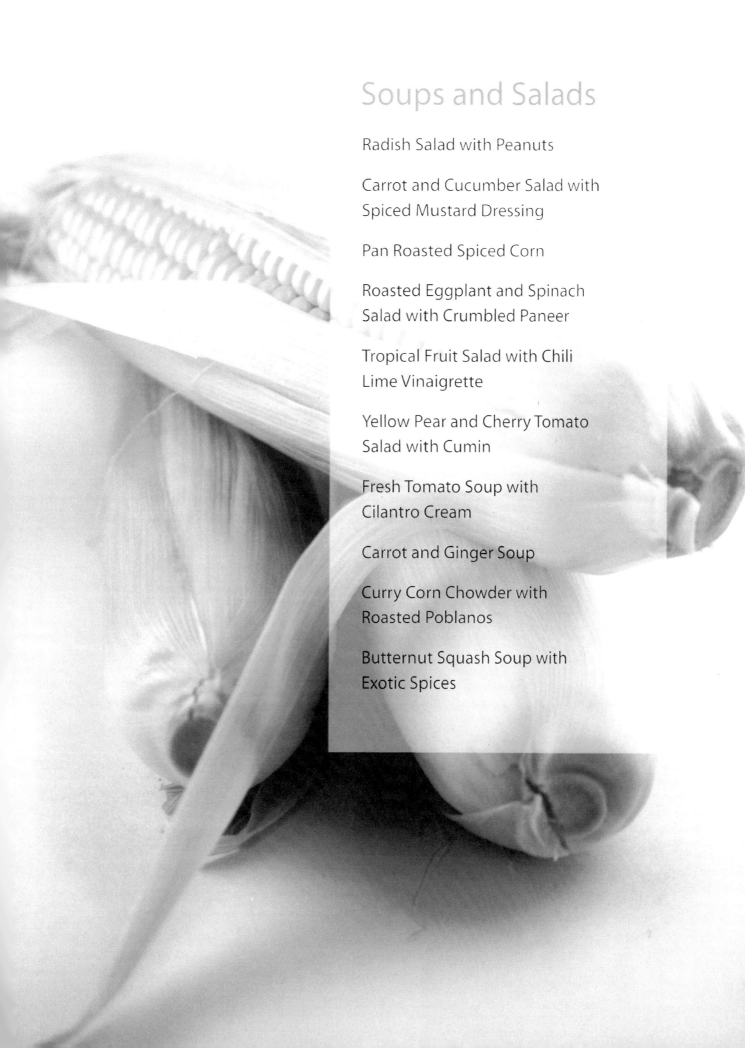

Soups and Salads

Radish Salad with Peanuts

Carrot and Cucumber Salad with
Spiced Mustard Dressing

Pan Roasted Spiced Corn

Roasted Eggplant and Spinach
Salad with Crumbled Paneer

Tropical Fruit Salad with Chili
Lime Vinaigrette

Yellow Pear and Cherry Tomato
Salad with Cumin

Fresh Tomato Soup with
Cilantro Cream

Carrot and Ginger Soup

Curry Corn Chowder with
Roasted Poblanos

Butternut Squash Soup with
Exotic Spices

Radish Salad with Peanuts

Serves 2

1 tablespoon olive oil
¼ teaspoon cumin seeds
¼ teaspoon black mustard seeds
1 small red onion, minced
¼ teaspoon ground turmeric
Salt to taste
1 tablespoon lemon juice
2 cups small red radishes, trimmed and sliced
1 cup peanuts, roasted and chopped
1 tablespoon cilantro, chopped

Heat the oil in a small saucepan over medium heat, add the cumin and mustard seeds, then cover and shake the saucepan until the seeds start to pop.

Add the onion, turmeric and salt to the saucepan, cook for a minute then remove from the heat. Add the lemon juice and radishes. Let cool completely.

Serve topped with peanuts and cilantro.

Carrot and Cucumber Salad with Spiced Mustard Dressing

Serves 4

4 tablespoons plain yogurt

2 tablespoons sesame seeds, toasted and ground

2 teaspoons cumin seeds, toasted and ground

½ pound cucumbers, peeled, seeded and diced

½ pound carrots, grated

Salt to taste

2 teaspoons mustard oil

½ teaspoon mustard seeds

½ teaspoon nigella seeds

1 green cayenne chili, slit lengthwise and seeded

¼ teaspoon cayenne pepper

¼ teaspoon turmeric

1 tablespoon fresh lemon juice

2 tablespoons mint leaves, minced

In a small bowl, add the yogurt, sesame and cumin and mix well to make a smooth paste. Add the cucumbers, carrots and salt. Set aside.

Heat the oil in a small skillet over medium heat. Add the mustard seeds, nigella seeds and chili and cook for about a minute, stirring until the spices are aromatic. Add the cayenne and turmeric. Stir and pour the flavored oil over the cucumbers; toss gently. Add the lemon juice and chill.

Serve cold topped with mint leaves.

Pan Roasted Spiced Corn

Serves 4

2 teaspoons cumin seeds
½ teaspoon fennel seeds
2 dried red chilies
1 pound frozen corn, thawed
2 tablespoons corn oil
1 small onion, finely chopped
Salt to taste
1 red bell pepper, finely chopped
3 tablespoons fresh cilantro, finely chopped
Mixed baby greens

In a small nonstick skillet, dry-roast the cumin, fennel and chilies over medium heat, stirring and shaking the skillet until the spices are fragrant and a few shades darker, about 2 minutes. Transfer to a bowl, let cool and grind finely in a mortar and pestle or in a spice grinder.

Place the corn in a nonstick skillet and stir over medium-high heat until the water evaporates. Transfer to a bowl.

In the same skillet, heat the oil over medium-high heat and cook the onion, stirring, until golden, 3 to 5 minutes. Add the corn, roasted spices and salt and cook until the corn is golden brown, 2 to 3 minutes.

Add the pepper and cilantro and cook about 2 minutes. Cool and serve over mixed baby greens.

Roasted Eggplant and Spinach Salad with Crumbled Paneer

Serves 4

1 tablespoon red wine vinegar

1 tablespoon fresh lemon juice

2 teaspoons chopped fresh mint

Salt to taste

1 teaspoon freshly ground pepper

3 tablespoons extra-virgin olive oil

1 large eggplant, diced

1 pound baby spinach

1 English cucumber, peeled, seeded and diced

1 tomato, seeded and diced

½ red onion, diced

½ red bell pepper, diced

4 tablespoons crumbled paneer cheese

Preheat the oven to 450°F. Lightly coat a baking sheet with olive oil.

In a small bowl, whisk together the vinegar, lemon juice, mint, salt and pepper. While whisking slowly add the olive oil in a thin stream until emulsified. Set aside.

Spread the eggplant cubes in a single layer on the prepared baking sheet. Spray the eggplant with olive oil cooking spray. Roast for 10 minutes. Turn the cubes and roast until softened and lightly golden, 8 to 10 minutes more. Set aside and let cool completely.

In a large bowl, combine the spinach, cucumber, tomato, onion, pepper and cooled eggplant. Pour the vinaigrette over the salad. Toss gently to mix well and coat evenly. Divide the salad among individual plates. Sprinkle with the paneer cheese. Serve immediately.

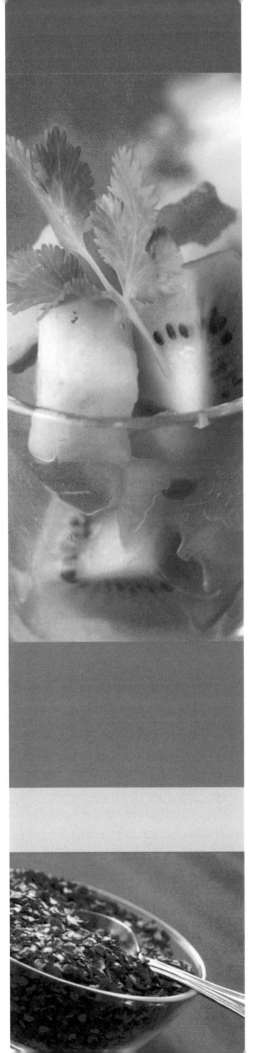

Tropical Fruit Salad with Chili Lime Vinaigrette

Serves 6

5 tablespoons white balsamic vinegar

3 tablespoons fresh lime juice

½ tablespoon sugar

Salt to taste

2 teaspoons red pepper flakes

½ cup extra-virgin olive oil

2 firm ripe mango's, peeled and cut into ½-inch cubes

1 pound pineapple, peeled, cored and cut into ½-inch cubes

1 medium red onion, thinly sliced

1 small red bell pepper, thinly sliced

1 cup cilantro leaves, chopped

Whisk together vinegar, lime juice, sugar, salt and red pepper flakes until sugar is dissolved. Add the oil in a thin stream, whisking until emulsified. Add remaining ingredients and toss until coated. Serve chilled.

Yellow Pear and Cherry Tomato Salad with Cumin

Serves 4

2 tablespoons lemon juice

2 tablespoons red onion, minced

2 teaspoons honey

2 tablespoons extra-virgin olive oil

Salt to taste

½ teaspoon red pepper flakes

2 teaspoons cumin seeds, toasted and coarsely ground

2 cups yellow pear tomatoes, halved

1 cup red cherry tomatoes, halved

1 cup orange cherry tomatoes, halved

1 tablespoon fresh basil, chopped

In a small bowl, combine the lemon juice, red onion, honey, olive oil, salt, red pepper flakes and cumin. Whisk until well-blended.

In a large salad bowl, toss together all the tomatoes. Pour the dressing on top, add the chopped basil and toss gently to mix well.

Southern Indian Potatoes with Peas and Tarragon

Fresh Tomato Soup with Cilantro Cream

Serves 4

2 teaspoons vegetable oil

½ small yellow onion, diced

1 bay leaf

4 medium tomatoes, peeled, seeded and diced

1 tablespoon tomato paste

1½ cups milk

Salt to taste

½ teaspoon freshly ground pepper

1 tablespoon cilantro, chopped

In a large heavy saucepan, heat the oil over medium heat. Add the onion and bay leaf and sauté until soft and translucent, about 4 minutes. Add the tomato and tomato paste and bring it to boil. Reduce the heat to medium low and simmer uncovered until the soup thickens about 15 to 20 minutes. Remove the bay leaf.

In a blender, purée the soup until smooth and return to the pan. Stir in the milk, salt, pepper and cilantro. Reheat gently. Ladle into individual bowls and serve hot with 1 tablespoon of cilantro cream in each bowl. Garnish with cilantro sprigs.

½ cup heavy cream

1 teaspoon finely chopped cilantro leaves

Salt and freshly ground pepper to taste

Whip the heavy cream, cilantro, salt and pepper until stiff peaks form. Refrigerate until ready to use.

Carrot and Ginger Soup

Serves 4

1 tablespoon vegetable oil

1 teaspoon mustard seeds

½ yellow onion, chopped

1 pound carrots, peeled and cut into ½-inch pieces

2 tablespoons ginger, minced

1 green chili, minced

2 teaspoons curry powder

5 cups vegetable stock or water

¼ cup Thai basil, chopped

2 tablespoons fresh lime juice

Salt to taste

3 tablespoons sour cream

Grated zest of lime

In a large saucepan, heat the oil over medium heat. Add the mustard seeds. When the seeds begin to pop, add the onions and sauté until soft and translucent. Add the carrots, ginger, green chili and curry powder and sauté until the seasonings are fragrant, about 3 minutes.

Add the stock, raise the heat to high and bring to a boil. Reduce the heat to medium low and simmer uncovered, until the carrots are tender, about 6 minutes.

In a blender, purée the soup until smooth and return to the saucepan. Reheat gently. Just before serving, stir in the chopped basil and lime juice. Season with salt.

Ladle into individual bowls. Garnish with a dollop of sour cream and lime zest.

Curry Corn Chowder with Roasted Poblanos

Serves 4

2 poblano chilies

1 pound of potatoes, peeled and diced into (1- inch) cubes

4 tablespoons vegetable oil

1 teaspoon cumin seeds

1 medium onion, chopped

¼ cup celery, diced

½ cup green bell pepper, diced

Salt to taste

3 cups fresh corn kernels or frozen corn, thawed

2 cups vegetable stock or water

1 cup cream

1 tablespoon curry powder

3 tablespoons cilantro, chopped

Preheat the grill or a broiler. Grill or broil the chilies until the skin begins to blacken, 5 to 7 minutes. Transfer to a bowl, cover with plastic wrap and let steam until the skin loosens, about 10 minutes. Peel the chilies and chop coarsely. Set aside.

In a small saucepan, add the potatoes and enough water to cover and cook until tender. Drain and set aside.

In a large saucepan, heat the oil, cumin, onion, celery and pepper and sauté until the vegetables are softened, about 5 minutes. Add salt and corn and cook for 3 to 4 minutes longer. Stir in the roasted chilies, potatoes, stock, cream, curry powder and 1 tablespoon of cilantro and simmer until the soup thickens, 20 to 25 minutes.

Serve hot garnished with the remaining cilantro.

Butternut Squash Soup with Exotic Spices

Serves 6

2 tablespoons unsalted butter

1 large onion, thinly sliced

2 bay leaves

2 star anise

1 cinnamon stick

1 tablespoon Madras curry powder

1 (1-inch) piece ginger, minced

3 cloves garlic, minced

2 pounds butternut squash, peeled and diced

Salt to taste

1 teaspoon freshly ground pepper

2 cups unsweetened coconut milk

4 cups unsalted vegetable stock or water

In a large saucepan, melt the butter over medium heat. Add the onion, bay leaves, star anise and cinnamon. Cook, stirring until the onions are tender, about 5 to 7 minutes. Add the curry powder, ginger and garlic and cook for 2 minutes. Add the squash, season with salt and pepper and sauté for 1 minute.

Stir in the coconut milk and stock. Bring to a boil and then reduce to a simmer. Cook, stirring occasionally, until the squash is tender, about 20 to 25 minutes. Remove the bay leaves, star anise and cinnamon stick.

Using blender or food processor, purée the soup working in batches until smooth. Strain through a fine sieve and season with salt and pepper if needed. Serve hot.

Vegetables

Oven Roasted Spiced Eggplant

Stir Fried Potatoes and Green Beans with Mint

Southern Indian Potatoes with Peas and Tarragon

Aromatic Butternut Squash and Coconut

Baby Beets and Carrots with Curry Leaves

Kadhai Fried Paneer with Rainbow Vegetables

Spice Stuffed Okra

Sweet and Sour Asparagus with Cashew Nuts

Paneer Picatta

Paneer Cheese

Zucchini with Yellow Mung Lentils and Roasted Garlic

Green Cabbage with Lentils

Spicy Puréed Spinach with Red Potatoes

Stuffed Tomatoes with Cilantro Coconut Cream Sauce

Mustard Potatoes with Dill

Oven Roasted Spiced Eggplant

Serves 6

4 medium purple Asian eggplants

½ cup vegetable oil

1 large onion, thinly sliced

1 teaspoon minced garlic

½ teaspoon cayenne pepper

½ teaspoon turmeric

½ teaspoon cumin seeds, toasted
and coarsely ground

2 tablespoons green chilies, minced

Salt to taste

2 tablespoons scallions, minced

¼ cup cilantro leaves for garnish

Preheat the oven to 450°F.

Cut the eggplant skin on into 1-inch dices. Lightly toss the eggplant with ¼ cup of oil and ½ teaspoon of salt. Place the eggplant on a baking sheet or roasting pan and bake in the center of the oven until lightly brown and the flesh is softened, about 10 minutes. Set the eggplant aside to cool.

Heat ¼ cup of oil in a heavy skillet over medium-high heat. Toss in the onion, garlic, cayenne, turmeric and cumin and stir to mix well. Lower the heat to medium and cook, stirring frequently, until the onion is soft and translucent but not browned, about 10 minutes.

Add the chilies to the onion mixture and sauté for about a minute then add the roasted eggplant and salt and combine ingredients using spatula.

Just before serving, stir in the scallions. Garnish with cilantro and serve hot or cold.

Stir Fried Potatoes and Green Beans with Mint

Serves 6

8 medium potatoes

½ pound green beans

3 tablespoons vegetable oil

1 tablespoon black mustard seeds

1 tablespoon cumin seeds

1 teaspoon turmeric

2 medium tomatoes, coarsely chopped

Salt to taste

2 green chilies, seeded and minced

4 scallions, minced

4 tablespoons mint leaves, chopped

Place the potatoes in a large pot with cold water to cover, bring to a boil and cook until just cooked through but still very firm (test the largest potato in the pot; it should be firm but cooked at the center). Drain. Set aside to cool.

Bring water to a boil in a medium pot. Toss in the green beans and cook until just tender, about 2 to 3 minutes. Drain, rinse under cold water to cool and then drain again. Trim into ½-inch lengths and set aside.

Peel the potatoes and chop into 1-inch dice. Set aside.

Heat the oil in a wok or a wide heavy pot over medium-high heat. When the oil is hot, toss in the mustard seeds. When they stop popping, add the cumin seeds and turmeric, stir briefly and then stir in the tomatoes and salt. Stir-fry for about 1 minute. Add the potatoes and stir-fry for a minute. Stir in the chilies, scallions, green beans and mint. Remove from the heat and season with salt if necessary.

Serve hot.

Southern Indian Potatoes with Peas and Terragon

Southern Indian Potatoes with Peas and Tarragon

Serves 6

1 pound small red or white potatoes

3 tablespoons vegetable oil

1 teaspoon black mustard seeds

1 tablespoon dried yellow split chickpeas

1 medium red onion, thinly sliced

1 tablespoon ground coriander

¼ teaspoon red pepper flakes

¼ teaspoon ground turmeric

2 tablespoons fresh curry leaves, minced

2 fresh green chilies, minced

1 cup frozen shelled peas, thawed

Salt to taste

½ cup fresh tarragon, chopped

Put the potatoes in a saucepan, add water to cover and bring to a boil over high heat. Reduce the heat to medium and cook, uncovered until the potatoes are tender, 15 to 20 minutes. Drain and let stand until cool. Cut each potato into quarters. Set aside.

Heat the oil in large nonstick wok or skillet over medium-high heat and add the mustard seeds and chickpeas; they will splutter upon contact with the oil, so cover the pan and reduce the heat until the spluttering subsides.

Quickly add the onion and cook, stirring, until golden, about 5 minutes. Then mix in the coriander, red pepper flakes, turmeric, curry leaves and chilies. Cook for 1 minute, add the potatoes, peas and salt. Cover and cook, stirring occasionally over medium-low heat until the potatoes are golden, 5 to 7 minutes. Add tarragon and transfer to a serving dish.

Aromatic Butternut Squash and Coconut

Serves 4

2 tablespoons vegetable oil

½ teaspoon cumin seeds

2 dried red chilies, stemmed

1 (1-inch) cinnamon stick

2 bay leaves

1 cup onion, chopped

1 pound butternut squash peeled, diced

1 teaspoon coriander seeds, ground

1 teaspoon brown sugar

Salt to taste

1 cup fresh or frozen grated coconut

¼ cup water

¼ cup cilantro, chopped

Heat the oil in a large heavy skillet over medium-high heat. Add the cumin, chilies, cinnamon, bay leaves and fry briefly. Add the onion and cook, stirring frequently, until golden brown, about 5 minutes. Add the squash lower the heat to medium and cook, stirring constantly to prevent sticking for 5 minutes. Add the coriander, brown sugar and salt and cook for 2 minutes, until the squash is soft.

Add the coconut and stir to break up lumps until blended into the squash. Add the water. Cook for 2 to 3 minutes, stirring to prevent sticking. Taste for seasonings and adjust if necessary. Garnish with cilantro.

Baby Beets and Carrots with Curry Leaves

Serves 6

1 pound red and yellow beets

½ pound baby carrots, peeled

1 tablespoon vegetable oil

8 fresh or frozen curry leaves

2 tablespoons green chilies, seeded and minced

3 tablespoons shallots, minced

1 tablespoon rice vinegar

Salt to taste

1 teaspoon sugar

If the beet greens are still attached, cut them off, leaving about 1 inch of stem intact. In a large pot, bring 1 inch of water to boil. Add the unpeeled beets, cover and cook until tender, 20 to 25 minutes. Remove from pot and let stand until cool enough to handle, then peel and cut into quarters. Set aside and keep warm.

Cook the carrots the same as the beets. (If the carrots are varied sizes, cut the larger ones into halves or thirds for even cooking). Remove from the pot and set aside.

Place a pan over medium-high heat. Add the oil and when it is hot, add the curry leaves, chilies and shallots. Cook for 2 to 3 minutes, stirring occasionally. Add the beets and carrots and stir, then add the vinegar, salt and sugar and stir to mix well. Raise the heat to high and stir-fry for 2 to 3 minutes.

Remove from the heat and taste for seasoning. Transfer to a serving dish; serve hot or at room temperature.

Kadhai Fried Paneer with Rainbow Vegetables

Kadhai Fried Paneer with Rainbow Vegetables

Serves 4

3 tablespoons vegetable oil

1 tablespoon ginger, minced

2 large cloves garlic, minced

2 small onions, diced

2 teaspoons ground coriander

1 teaspoon ground cumin

½ teaspoon ground fennel seeds

½ teaspoon ground cardamom seeds

½ teaspoon red pepper flakes

Salt to taste

4 small tomatoes, diced

2 small green bell peppers, diced

2 small red bell peppers, diced

2 small yellow bell peppers, diced

6 ounces paneer cheese, diced

½ cup fresh cilantro, chopped

4 scallions, chopped

Freshly ground black pepper

Heat the oil in a large nonstick wok or skillet over medium-high heat; add the ginger and garlic, stirring about 1 minute. Add the onions and cook, stirring until golden, 2 to 3 minutes.

Add the coriander, cumin, fennel, cardamom and red pepper flakes and stir over medium heat, about 2 minutes. Add the tomatoes and bell peppers, cover the wok and continue to cook, stirring constantly until the dish is saucy, about 5 minutes.

Add the paneer, cilantro and scallions and cook over medium-high heat, uncovered, about 5 minutes.

Serve hot, sprinkled with black pepper.

Spice Stuffed Okra

Serves 6

1 tablespoon ground coriander

1 teaspoon ground cumin

1 teaspoon mango powder

1 teaspoon ground fennel seeds

½ teaspoon ground turmeric

½ teaspoon garam masala

½ teaspoon ground paprika

½ teaspoon chili powder

Salt to taste

1½ pounds fresh tender okra, rinsed and patted dry

3 tablespoons vegetable oil

1½ teaspoons cumin seeds

1 large onion, cut in half lengthwise and thinly sliced

1 large tomato, coarsely chopped

In a small bowl, mix together the first eight spices and salt.

Remove the ends of the okra stems and discard. Make a long slit on one side from the stem down, stopping ½-inch from the tip. (This forms a pocket for the stuffing, but keeps the okra intact). Stuff ½ teaspoon of the spice mixture into each okra pocket. Reserve any leftover spice mixture.

Heat 2 tablespoons of oil in flat nonstick skillet and add the cumin seeds, they should sizzle upon contact with the hot oil. Quickly add the onion and cook, stirring, over medium-high heat until golden, about 5 minutes. With a slotted spatula, transfer to a bowl, leaving behind any oil.

Lay the stuffed okra in the skillet in a single layer. Drizzle the remaining 1 tablespoon of oil on top and cook over medium-low heat, turning the pieces very carefully, until golden brown, about 10 to 15 minutes. Scatter the cooked onions over the okras and then add any leftover spices. Mix carefully and cook over medium-low heat, turning occasionally, about 5 minutes. Transfer to a serving platter.

Add the tomatoes to the skillet and cook over high heat until wilted and coated with any spices left in the skillet, about 2 minutes. Transfer to the platter and serve.

Sweet and Sour Asparagus with Cashew Nuts

Serves 6

1 pound asparagus, trimmed and cut into 2-inch pieces

3 tablespoons vegetable oil

½ teaspoon cumin seeds

½ teaspoon mustard seeds

2 small onions, sliced

1 tablespoon fresh ginger, minced

1 large clove fresh garlic, minced

2 fresh green chili peppers, chopped without the seeds

1 tablespoon ground coriander

½ teaspoon ground cumin

Salt to taste

1 large tomato, coarsely chopped

¼ cup nonfat plain yogurt, whisked until smooth

½ cup cashew nuts, roasted and coarsely chopped

¼ teaspoon garam masala

Precook the asparagus in boiling water or in a microwave for about 2 to 3 minutes, shock in cold water and set aside.

Heat the oil in a medium nonstick wok or saucepan over medium-high heat and then add the cumin and mustard seeds; they should sizzle upon contact with the hot oil. Quickly add the onions and cook, stirring until golden brown, about 5 minutes.

Add the ginger, garlic and green chili and stir about 1 minute, then add the coriander, cumin and salt and stir.

Add the tomato and cook until lightly soft, about 1 minute.

Add the yogurt, stirring constantly to prevent it from curdling, about 2 minutes.

Add the asparagus and cook until the flavors are well-blended for about 2 minutes.

Serve garnished with roasted cashew nuts and sprinkle garam masala on top.

Paneer Picatta

Paneer Picatta

Serves 4

8 ounces paneer cheese
Salt to taste
Freshly ground black pepper
1 tablespoon vegetable oil
¼ cup sherry or dry white wine
1 small onion, minced
¼ cup drained capers
1 tablespoon ginger, minced
2 fresh green chili peppers, minced
Juice of 1 lemon
2 tablespoons butter
½ cup fresh cilantro, chopped

Season the paneer lightly with salt and black pepper.

Heat the oil in a large nonstick skillet or griddle over medium-high heat and quickly sear the cheese until golden, about 1 minute per side. Transfer to a serving dish, cover and keep warm.

Add the sherry to deglaze the pan, scraping the browned bits off the bottom.

Add the onions, capers, ginger and chili peppers and cook, stirring for about 2 minutes.

Add the lemon juice, butter and cilantro then drizzle everything over the cheese and serve hot.

Paneer Cheese

Makes ½ pound

Paneer, which is also known as Indian cottage cheese, is made by curdling milk with something sour, such as yogurt, lemon juice or vinegar and then separating the curds from the whey.

This soft, spongy cheese with its sweet, milky aroma is preservative-free, has no artificial additives and can be made with low fat or whole milk.

Paneer cheese can be served as part of an antipasto platter, giving it an Italian twist with salt, pepper, chopped fresh basil and balsamic vinegar or as a caprese salad with fresh plum tomatoes and basil.

½ gallon low fat or whole milk

½ cup fresh lemon juice

1 (2-foot-square) piece of fine muslin or layers of cheesecloth

Place the milk in a large, heavy saucepan and bring to a boil, stirring constantly, over medium-high heat. Just before the milk boils, add the lemon juice and continue to stir until the milk curdles and separates into curds and whey, 1 to 2 minutes. Remove from the heat.

Let sit for 5 minutes.

Drape the muslin or cheesecloth over a large pan and pour the curdled milk over it. As you do this, the whey drains through the cloth into the pan and the curdled paneer cheese remains in the cloth.

Tie the ends of the cloth and hang over a sink. Allow to drain 3 to 5 minutes.

Twist the cloth around the cheese, then place the cheese between 2 plates. Place a large pan of water or a heavy saucepan on the top plate and let the cheese drain further, 10 to 20 minutes.

Remove the weight off the cheese (which, by now, should have compressed into a chunk), cut into desired shapes and sizes and use as needed. Store in an airtight container in the refrigerator 4 to 5 days or freeze up to 4 months.

Variations

Paneer cheese can also be made with 1 cup fresh chopped herbs like basil, tarragon or mint.

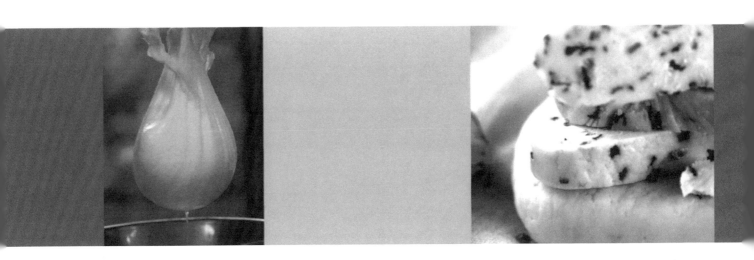

Zucchini with Yellow Mung Lentils and Roasted Garlic

Serves 6

1 cup yellow mung lentils, rinsed and drained

½ teaspoon turmeric

Salt to taste

4 cups water

2 tablespoons oil

6 cloves garlic, crushed

1 teaspoon cumin seeds

1 small onion, thinly sliced

4 small zucchinis, cut into ½-inch slices

1 tablespoon ground coriander

1 tablespoon ground cumin

½ teaspoon paprika

2 tablespoons cilantro, chopped

Put the lentils into a large saucepan with turmeric, salt and water. Bring to a boil and skim well. Reduce the heat and simmer, covered, until the lentils are cooked, about 15 to 20 minutes. Transfer to a serving bowl. Cover bowl and keep warm.

In a medium saucepan, heat 2 tablespoons of oil, add the garlic and cook until golden brown and well roasted.

Add the cumin seeds. They should sizzle upon contact with the hot oil. Quickly add the onions and zucchini and cook for 10 to 15 minutes over medium heat.

Add coriander and cumin and cook for 10 minutes or until the zucchini is cooked.

Remove the pan form the heat, add the paprika and immediately pour over the hot lentils and stir lightly to mix. Sprinkle the cilantro on top and serve.

Green Cabbage with Lentils

Green Cabbage with Lentils

Serves 6

2 tablespoons vegetable oil

1½ teaspoons cumin seeds

2 tablespoons dried curry leaves

1 tablespoon fresh ginger, minced

1 tablespoon fresh garlic, minced

2 fresh green chilies, minced

1 teaspoon ground coriander

*1 small head green cabbage (about 1½ pounds),
finely shredded*

1 cup dried lentils, washed and cooked

Salt to taste

½ cup fresh cilantro, including soft stems, chopped

¼ teaspoon garam masala

Heat the oil in a large saucepan over medium-high heat and add the cumin seeds and curry leaves, they should sizzle upon contact with the hot oil. Quickly add the ginger, garlic, chilies, and coriander and cook, stirring, about 2 minutes

Add the cabbage and salt, cover the pan and cook, stirring as needed, over medium-high heat for first 2 to 3 minutes and then over medium-low heat until the cabbage is tender, about 10 minutes. Mix in the cooked lentils and cilantro during the last 5 minutes. Transfer to a serving bowl, sprinkle the garam masala and serve.

Spicy Puréed Spinach with Red Potatoes

Serves 4

2 (1-inch) peeled fresh ginger pieces

2 cloves garlic, peeled

2 green chili peppers

1 pound spinach, chopped, fresh or frozen

1 cup water

2 tablespoons vegetable oil

1 teaspoon cumin seeds

1 medium onion, finely chopped

1 pound red potatoes, diced

1 tablespoon ground coriander

1 teaspoon garam masala

½ teaspoon paprika

Salt to taste

2 medium tomatoes, chopped

In a food processor or a blender, add the ginger, garlic and chili peppers until minced. Add the spinach and water, process again to make a coarse purée.

Heat the oil in a large nonstick saucepan over medium-high heat and add the cumin seeds, quickly add the onion and sauté, stirring until golden. Add the potatoes and stir for about 3 minutes.

Mix in the coriander, garam masala, paprika and salt. Add the tomatoes and cook, stirring for about 5 minutes.

Mix in the puréed spinach and cook, stirring, until it comes to a boil and the potatoes are cooked about 10 minutes and serve hot.

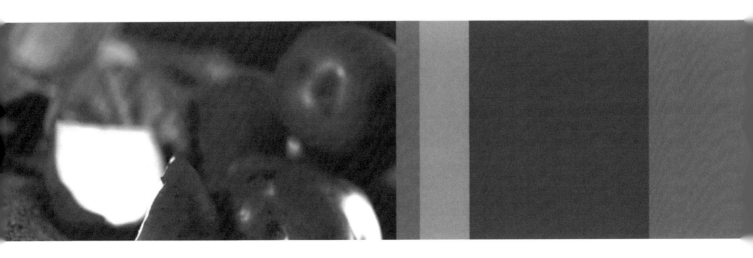

Stuffed Tomatoes with Cilantro Coconut Cream Sauce

Serves 6

2 large firm tomatoes

4 small potatoes, boiled, skinned and mashed

1 cup paneer cheese, grated

¼ cup cheddar cheese, grated

2 tablespoons fresh cilantro, finely chopped

1 tablespoon ginger, minced

1 fresh green chili pepper, minced

1 tablespoon ground coriander

Salt to taste

2 tablespoons vegetable oil

1 teaspoon cumin seeds

1 teaspoon turmeric

Sauce

1 medium onion, finely chopped

4 cloves garlic

4 cardamom pods, crushed

1 tablespoon ginger, minced

1 cinnamon stick

1 teaspoon ground coriander

1 teaspoon cumin

¼ teaspoon turmeric

½ teaspoon chili powder

1 cup coconut milk

1 cup fresh cilantro, chopped

Cut a small circle around the stem of each tomato and carefully remove the top, to make a cap. Remove the membranes and the seeds from inside each tomato.

In a medium bowl, mix together the mashed potato, paneer and cheddar cheese, cilantro, ginger, chili pepper, coriander and salt.

Heat the oil in a large nonstick skillet over medium-high heat and add the cumin seeds and turmeric, they should sizzle upon contact with the hot oil. Quickly add the potato mixture and cook, stirring, about 5 minutes. Divide the potato mixture equally among the tomatoes and fill each one.

To make the sauce, combine all the sauce ingredients in a large, heavy-bottomed frying pan and bring slowly to a boil. Reduce the heat to low, cover and simmer for 20 minutes. Season with salt to taste.

Add the stuffed tomatoes to the sauce, arranging them so that they stand upright in a single layer and cook for another 5 minutes, or until the sauce is thick. Serve the tomatoes with a little sauce over the top.

Mustard Potatoes with Dill

Mustard Potatoes with Dill

Serves 6

1 pound potatoes, diced
4 tablespoons vegetable oil
5 cloves garlic , minced
2 teaspoons black mustard seeds
2 dried red chilies, whole
1 tablespoon Madras curry powder
6 cups dill, rinsed and chopped
Salt to taste

Boil the potatoes in a saucepan, over medium-high heat, simmer for 10 to 15 minutes or until just tender. Drain well.

Heat the oil in a heavy-bottomed saucepan over medium-high heat. Add the garlic and fry for 30 seconds. Add the mustard seeds and the chilies, cover and briefly allow the seeds to pop. Stir in the potatoes with the curry powder and sauté until fragrant. Add the dill, cover and cook over low heat for 5 minutes. Season with salt and serve hot.

Beans and Legumes

Black-Eyed Peas with Mushrooms

Hot & Sour Chickpeas

Cannellini Dal Fry

Spicy Red Lentils

Chickpeas with Spinach and
Fingerling Potatoes

Madras Style Lentils and
Vegetable Stew

Street Style Spicy Black
Chickpea Masala

Red Bean Ragout with Plum
Tomatoes and Thyme

Yellow Lentils with Baby Spinach
and Garlic

Masala Petit Pois with Baby Carrots
and Coconut

Black-Eyed Peas with Mushrooms

Serves 6

1 cup dried black-eyed peas

4 cups water

½ teaspoon salt

½ cup vegetable oil

1 teaspoon cumin seeds

1 (1-inch) cinnamon stick

1 cup red onions, chopped

4 cloves garlic , minced

½ pound button mushrooms, cleaned and sliced

1 pound ripe tomatoes, blanched and chopped

2 teaspoons ground coriander

1 teaspoon ground cumin

½ teaspoon ground turmeric

¼ teaspoon paprika

Salt to taste

2 tablespoons fresh cilantro, chopped

In a large saucepan over high heat, combine the peas, water and salt. Bring to a boil. Cover and simmer until the peas are tender, about 45 minutes.

Drain, rinse with cold water, drain again and transfer to a large bowl to cool.

Heat the oil in a heavy-bottomed frying pan or saucepan. Add the cumin seeds and cinnamon stick, let them sizzle for 10 seconds. Add the onions and garlic. Stir over medium heat until soft and starting to brown, about 5 minutes. Add the mushroom and fry for 2 to 3 minutes. Add the tomatoes, coriander, cumin, turmeric, paprika and salt. Cover and cook over low heat for 10 minutes.

Add the peas to the tomato and mushroom mixture and season with salt to taste. Stir in the cilantro and simmer, uncovered, for 10 minutes.

Hot and Sour Chickpeas

Serves 6

1 tablespoon ground dried
pomegranate seeds

2 teaspoons ground cumin

1 teaspoon dried mango powder

½ teaspoon garam masala

½ teaspoon dark chili powder

3 tablespoons vegetable oil

1 tablespoon fresh ginger, minced

2 tablespoons fresh garlic, minced

2 fresh green chili peppers, minced

1 tablespoon ground coriander

1 pound canned chickpeas, drained and rinsed well

Salt to taste

½ cup water

1 teaspoon cumin seeds

1 (1-inch) peeled fresh ginger,
cut into thin matchsticks

1 small red onion, sliced

2 small tomatoes, diced

½ cup fresh cilantro, chopped

Place the pomegranate seeds, cumin, mango powder, garam masala and chili powder in a small skillet and toast, stirring constantly over medium heat until fragrant and slightly brown, about 2 minutes.

Heat 2 tablespoons of oil in a large saucepan over medium-high heat and add the ginger, garlic and chili peppers, stirring, until golden, about 1 minute. Add the coriander and mix in the chickpeas, salt and water and cook, stirring as needed until tender and almost dry, about 5 minutes. Add the roasted spices, reduce the heat to medium and cook another 5 minutes to blend the flavors. Transfer to a serving dish and keep warm.

Heat the remaining oil in a small saucepan over medium-high heat and add the cumin seeds; they should sizzle upon contact with the hot oil. Quickly add the ginger and then add the onions and tomato and cook until golden. Stir about 1 minute and add to the chickpeas.

Garnish with cilantro and serve hot.

Cannellini Dal Fry

Serves 6

1 cup cannellini beans, washed, soaked overnight and drained
6 cups water
Salt to taste
2 bay leaves
1 (1-inch) stick cinnamon
3 tablespoons vegetable oil
1 clove garlic, minced
1½ teaspoons cumin seeds
2 large tomatoes, finely chopped
2 fresh green chilies, minced
1½ tablespoons fresh ginger, minced
2 tablespoons ground coriander
1 teaspoon ground cumin
½ teaspoon ground turmeric
½ cup nonfat plain yogurt, whisked until smooth
½ cup fresh cilantro, finely chopped
¼ teaspoon garam masala

In a large saucepan over high heat, combine the beans, water, salt, bay leaves and cinnamon. Bring to a boil. Reduce the heat to low and continue to cook and simmer until the beans are tender, about 50 to 60 minutes. Drain.

In a large saucepan, heat the oil over medium-high heat and cook the garlic until golden, about 1 minute. Add the cumin seeds; they should sizzle upon contact with the hot oil. Add the tomatoes, chilies and ginger and cook, stirring constantly, initially over high and then over medium heat until all the juices evaporate, about 10 minutes.

Add the coriander, cumin and turmeric and cook, stirring for 1 minute. Add the yogurt, a little at a time, stirring constantly to prevent it from curdling, until it is absorbed. Mix in the beans and cilantro and simmer for another 10 to 15 minutes, uncovered, adding more water, if necessary. Transfer to a serving dish, sprinkle with garam masala and serve.

Spicy Red Lentils

Serves 6

1 cup red lentils, rinsed and drained

4 cups water

¼ teaspoon ground turmeric

1 bay leaf

Salt to taste

2 tablespoons vegetable oil

1 small onion, finely chopped

½ tablespoon ginger, minced

½ tablespoon garlic, minced

1 fresh green chili pepper,
minced with seeds

1 tablespoon ground coriander

½ teaspoon ground cumin

¼ teaspoon ground cinnamon

1 teaspoon paprika

1 teaspoon sugar

3 tablespoons fresh cilantro, chopped

3 tablespoons fresh mint, chopped

2 tablespoons fresh lemon juice

In a saucepan over high heat, combine the lentils, water, turmeric, bay leaf and salt. Bring to a boil. Reduce the heat to medium and cook the lentils, stirring occasionally and simmer until tender but firm, 12 to 15 minutes. Drain.

In a small frying pan, heat the oil over medium heat. Add the onion, ginger, garlic, chili pepper, coriander, cumin, cinnamon, paprika and sugar. Reduce the heat to low and cook until fragrant, about 2 minutes. Remove the pan from the heat.

In a large bowl, combine the lentils and the spice mixture, toss gently to mix. Stir in cilantro and mint. Stir in the lemon juice and serve immediately.

Chickpeas with Spinach and Fingerling Potatoes

Serves 6

1 pound fingerling potatoes
Salt to taste
3 tablespoons vegetable oil
2 teaspoons cumin seeds
1 large onion, chopped
¼ teaspoon ground turmeric
½ tablespoon crushed red chili flakes
1 tablespoon ginger, minced
1 tablespoon garlic, minced
1 pound fresh spinach, trimmed, rinsed and chopped
1 pound canned chickpeas, drained and rinsed well
1½ cups water
½ cup fresh cilantro, finely chopped
1 tablespoon ground coriander
2 small tomatoes, cut into 6 wedges each

Boil the potatoes in lightly salted water to cover until soft, about 20 minutes. Cool and then cut into 1-inch pieces. In a large saucepan, heat the oil over medium-high heat and add the cumin seeds, they should sizzle upon contact with the hot oil. Quickly add the onions and turmeric and stir over medium heat until slightly brown, about 3 minutes.

Add the red chili flakes, ginger and garlic and stir for 1 minute. Then add the spinach and cook, stirring until wilted, about 3 minutes. Add the potatoes, chickpeas, water and cilantro and bring to a boil over high heat. Cover the pan, reduce the heat to medium and cook until the chickpeas are well-blended and fragrant, about 5 minutes. Mix in the coriander and cook for another 3 minutes.

Serve hot garnished with tomato wedges.

Madras Style Lentils and Vegetable Stew

Serves 6

1 cup lentils, rinsed and drained

6 cups water

½ teaspoon turmeric

4 tablespoons vegetable oil

2 fresh green chilies, split lengthwise

1 teaspoon black mustard seeds

¼ cup coconut, grated

2 tablespoons fresh curry leaves, minced

1 tablespoon ginger, minced

1 clove garlic, minced

Salt to taste

4 cups mixed fresh vegetables,
such as carrots, eggplant, green beans,
and summer squash, cut into 1-inch pieces

¼ cup fresh cilantro, chopped

In a large saucepan, add the lentils, water and turmeric and bring to a boil over high heat. Reduce the heat to low, cover the saucepan and cook, stirring occasionally, until soft and creamy, 25 to 30 minutes. Stir vigorously to mash the lentils. Keep warm.

Heat 2 tablespoons of oil in a medium saucepan over medium-high heat and add the green chilies, mustard seeds, coconut and curry leaves. Add the ginger and garlic and cook about 2 minutes. Pour it into the mashed lentils.

To the same pan, add the remaining 2 tablespoons of oil, vegetables and salt and cook, stirring, over medium-high heat until tender, about 8 to 10 minutes. Add the lentils and cook, stirring occasionally about 10 minutes to blend the flavors. Add more water if needed.

Serve hot, garnished with cilantro.

Street Style Spicy Black Chickpea Masala

Serves 4

1½ cups dried black chickpeas, rinsed, soaked overnight and drained

5 cups water

Salt to taste

3 tablespoons clarified butter

1 teaspoon cumin seeds

2 medium onions, chopped

1 tablespoon ginger, minced

3 fresh green chilies, minced

1 cup tomatoes, finely chopped

5 scallions, finely chopped

1 tablespoon ground coriander

½ teaspoon dark red chili powder

1 tablespoon garam masala

¼ cup fresh cilantro, chopped

1 small red onion, sliced thinly

3 to 4 lime wedges for garnish

In a large saucepan over high heat, combine the chickpeas, water and salt. Bring to a boil. Reduce the heat to low, cover partially and simmer until the chickpeas are tender, about 45 minutes. Drain and reserve.

In a large saucepan, heat the clarified butter over medium-high heat and add the cumin seeds; they should sizzle upon contact with the hot oil. Add the chopped onions and cook until dark golden brown, stirring frequently to prevent sticking. Add water if necessary.

Add the ginger, chilies, tomatoes and scallions, cook for about 3 to 5 minutes. Mix in the coriander, chili powder and garam masala.

Add the chickpeas and cook on high heat until all the water evaporates and the chickpeas are glazed with a dark brown coating, about 10 to 15 minutes. Serve topped with cilantro, onions and lime wedges.

Red Bean Ragout with Plum Tomatoes and Thyme

Serves 6

2 tablespoons vegetable oil

1 teaspoon cumin seeds

2 medium onions, minced

1½ teaspoons fresh thyme, chopped

2 teaspoons ginger, minced

4 cloves garlic, minced

2 fresh green chilies, minced

2 large plum tomatoes, chopped

2 teaspoons ground coriander

1 teaspoon ground cumin

¼ teaspoon turmeric

1 teaspoon garam masala

1 pound canned kidney beans, drained and rinsed

2 cups water

Salt to taste

2 sprigs thyme

In a large saucepan, heat the oil over medium–high heat, add the cumin seeds and let them sizzle. Add the onion and thyme and cook stirring frequently until the onions begin to brown, about 5 minutes.

Add the ginger, garlic, chilies, tomatoes, coriander, cumin, turmeric and garam masala and fry until the oil separates, about 5 minutes.

Add the beans, 2 cups of water, salt to taste and cook until beans are tender and the flavors are well-blended, about 10 minutes. Mash some of the beans roughly, to thicken the sauce.

Transfer to a serving bowl and serve garnished with thyme sprigs.

Yellow Lentils with Baby Spinach and Garlic

Serves 6

1 tablespoon vegetable oil

1 teaspoon mustard seeds

1 medium onion, chopped

2 cloves garlic, crushed

1 teaspoon ground ginger

1 teaspoon Madras curry powder

1 cup yellow lentils, rinsed and drained

1½ cups water

½ cup coconut milk

3 cups baby spinach, chopped or 1 cup frozen chopped spinach

Salt to taste

1 tablespoon fresh cilantro, chopped

1 teaspoon black sesame seeds

In a large saucepan, heat the oil over medium heat. Add the mustard seeds; they should sizzle upon contact with the hot oil. Add the onion, garlic, ginger, curry powder and cook, stirring until the spices are fragrant, about 1 minute.

Add the lentils, water and coconut milk. Raise the heat to medium-high and bring to a boil. Reduce the heat to low, cover partially and simmer until the lentils are tender but still firm, about 15 minutes.

Stir in the spinach and salt, cover and simmer for about 3 more minutes.

Serve hot, garnished with cilantro and sesame seeds.

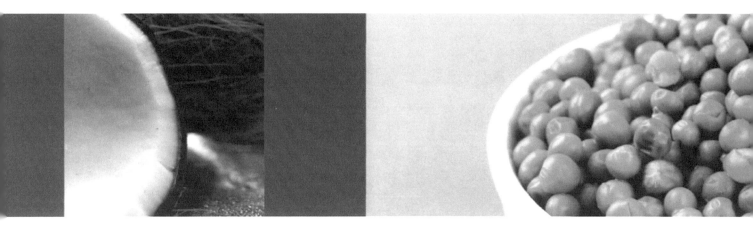

Masala Petit Pois with Baby Carrots and Coconut

Serves 6

1 pound fresh or frozen petit peas

5 tablespoons vegetable oil

1 pound baby carrots, diced

¼ cup water

¾ cup coconut, grated

¼ cup cashew nuts

2 teaspoons cumin seeds

1 teaspoon mustard seeds

1 medium onion, chopped

1 tablespoon ginger, minced

1 clove garlic, minced

2 teaspoons ground coriander

1 teaspoon red chili powder

1 teaspoon turmeric

Salt to taste

1 medium tomato, chopped

5 curry leaves

2 cups water

3 tablespoons fresh cilantro, chopped

In a large saucepan boil the peas with enough water until tender and soft. Drain.

If using the frozen peas, thaw.

Heat 2 tablespoons of oil in a large saucepan over medium-high heat, sauté the carrots for 3 minutes. Set aside.

In a blender, add water, coconut and cashews and make a fine paste.

In a large saucepan, heat remaining oil, over medium-high heat. Add cumin seeds and mustard seeds, sauté until fragrant, about 1 minute.

Add the onions, ginger and garlic and sauté until light brown. Add the coriander, chili powder, turmeric and salt, stir, add tomatoes and sauté until the fat leaves the mixture. About 5 minutes.

Reduce the heat, add the coconut cashew paste and the curry leaves, stir for a minute.

Add water and bring to a boil. Add peas and carrots, simmer for 5 minutes.

Serve hot, garnished with cilantro.

Rice

Tamarind Rice with
Roasted Peanuts

Lamb Pulao

Basmati Rice with
Dry-Roasted Spices

Saffron Rice with
Toasted Almonds

Mint Pilaf with Potatoes
and Cumin

Rosemary Lemon Rice

Spicy Eggplant Rice with Mint

Brown Basmati with Caramelized
Onions and Broccoli

Stir-Fried Mushrooms and
Red Chard Pilaf

Cranberry Pilaf

Layered Saffron Rice and
Chicken Casserole

Wild Rice Pilaf with Walnuts

Tamarind Rice with Roasted Peanuts

Serves 6

¼ cup hot water

2 tablespoons tamarind paste

3 tablespoons vegetable oil

1 teaspoon black mustard seeds

4 dried red chilies, roughly chopped

1 cup shallot, chopped

2 green chilies, coarsely chopped

¼ teaspoon turmeric

10 fresh curry leaves

4 cups basmati rice, cooked and cooled or at room temperature

Salt to taste

¼ cup cilantro leaves, chopped

2 tablespoons roasted peanuts for garnish

Pour the hot water over the tamarind paste in a bowl. Use a fork to combine the tamarind paste with the water and set aside.

Heat the oil in a large saucepan over medium-high heat. Add the mustard seeds. Cover loosely until the seeds have spluttered and popped for 10 to 15 seconds, and add the red chilies and shallots. Lower the heat to medium and stir-fry for about a minute.

Add the green chilies and turmeric. Stir-fry for about 2 minutes, until the chilies start to soften, then toss in the curry leaves and stir.

Add the rice to the mixture. Season it with salt, raise heat to high and stir-fry for 3 to 4 minutes. Add the tamarind liquid and fry for a few minutes, tossing the mixture to avoid lumps.

Serve hot, garnished with cilantro and peanuts.

Lamb Pulao

Serves 6

1½ pounds boneless lamb (shoulder cut),
cut into 1-inch cubes

Salt to taste

2 teaspoons garam masala

6 tablespoons vegetable oil or clarified butter

2 (2-inch) cinnamon sticks

1 teaspoon cumin seeds

6 cloves, whole

5 cardamom pods

2 bay leaves

1 teaspoon black peppercorns

2 tablespoons garlic, minced

3 tablespoons ginger, minced

3 cups onions, thinly sliced

2 teaspoons ground coriander

1½ teaspoons ground cumin

½ teaspoon mace powder

½ teaspoon freshly grated nutmeg

½ teaspoon cayenne pepper

1 cup fresh tomatoes, diced

1 teaspoon turmeric

1½ teaspoons salt

3 cups water

2 cups basmati rice, soaked, rinsed and drained

½ cup sliced almonds, toasted

Preheat the oven to 325°F

Place the lamb in a large bowl and season it with salt and garam masala. Set aside, covered, for 30 minutes.

In a wide, heavy, ovenproof pot with a tight-fitting lid, heat the oil or clarified butter over medium-high heat. Add the cinnamon, cumin seeds, cloves, cardamom, bay leaves and peppercorns and stir until fragrant. Add the garlic and ginger and stir-fry for 2 to 3 minutes, until aromatic. Add the onions and cook, stirring frequently, until very soft, 8 to 10 minutes.

Lower the heat and add coriander, cumin, mace, nutmeg, cayenne pepper and stir-fry for an additional minute.

Add the lamb and sear until browned. Add the tomatoes, turmeric and salt and stir. Add the water and bring to a boil.

Add the rice and bring back to a vigorous boil, about 5 minutes. Cover tightly (wrap the pot lid with foil if necessary to make a better seal) and place in the oven for 45 minutes.

Remove from the oven and let stand for 15 minutes, still covered. This will help to absorb all the flavors into the lamb.

Serve hot, garnished with the toasted almonds.

Basmati Rice with Dry-Roasted Spices

Serves 6

1½ teaspoons cumin seeds

1 teaspoon cloves, whole

½ teaspoon black peppercorns

5 to 7 green cardamom pods

*1½ cups basmati rice, washed in
3 to 4 changes of water and drained*

1 tablespoon oil or clarified butter

2½ cups water

Salt to taste

4 tablespoons finely chopped fresh mint

Place the cumin seeds, cloves, peppercorns and cardamom in a medium saucepan and roast, stirring and shaking the pan, over medium-high heat until highly fragrant, about 1 minute. Add the drained rice and oil or clarified butter and continue to roast another 1 to 3 minutes, stirring without breaking the grains of the rice.

Add the water and salt and bring to a boil over high heat. Reduce heat to the lowest setting, cover the pan and cook until the rice is done, 10 to 15 minutes. Do not stir the rice while it cooks. Remove from heat and let the rice rest for 5 minutes.

Transfer to a serving platter, garnish with mint and serve.

Saffron Rice with Toasted Almonds

Serves 4

½ teaspoon saffron threads

¼ cup warm milk

2 tablespoons vegetable oil

1 tablespoon ginger, minced

1 teaspoon cumin seeds

6 green cardamom pods

½ teaspoon black peppercorns

1 cup basmati rice, sorted and washed in
3 to 4 changes of water

2 cups water

Salt to taste

¼ teaspoon garam masala

½ cup sliced almonds, toasted

Soak the saffron in the milk about 15 minutes.

Heat the oil in a large nonstick saucepan over medium-high heat and sauté the ginger, cumin, cardamom and peppercorns, about 1 minute. Add the rice with the water and season it with salt and bring to a boil over high heat. Reduce the heat to lowest setting, cover the pan (partially at first, until the foam subsides, then snugly) and cook until the rice is almost done, 8 to 10 minutes.

Uncover the pan, sprinkle the saffron milk over the rice, then cover the pan and cook another 5 minutes to blend the flavors. Do not stir while the rice is cooking.

Serve hot, sprinkled with garam masala and toasted almonds.

Mint Pilaf with Potatoes and Cumin

Mint Pilaf with Potatoes and Cumin

Serves 6

2 tablespoons vegetable oil

1 small onion, thinly sliced

1 small potato, peeled and cut into ½-inch dices

1½ tablespoons fresh ginger, minced

2 tablespoons fresh mint leaves, minced

1 fresh green chili, minced

1¼ cups basmati rice, soaked, rinsed and drained

2¼ cups water

Salt to taste

3 teaspoons cumin seeds, roasted and crushed coarsely

Heat the oil in a large saucepan over medium-high heat and sauté the onion until brown, about 5 to 7 minutes. Add the potato, ginger, half the mint and the chili and cook, stirring, about 2 minutes.

Add the rice and sauté for 3 minutes. Add the water and the salt. Bring to a boil over high heat. Reduce the heat to the lowest setting, cover the pan and cook until the rice is done, 10 to 15 minutes. Do not stir the rice while it cooks. Remove from the heat and let the rice rest for about 5 minutes.

Transfer to a serving platter, sprinkle with roasted cumin and remaining mint leaves and serve.

Rosemary Lemon Rice

Serves 6

1½ cups long grain white rice

2 sprigs rosemary

2 teaspoons lemon zest

3 cups water

¼ teaspoon turmeric

Salt to taste

2 tablespoons fresh lemon juice

2 tablespoons vegetable oil

1½ teaspoons mustard seeds

1 teaspoon red chili flakes

2 (1-inch) cinnamon sticks

2 cloves, whole

Pour the rice, rosemary, lemon zest, water, turmeric and salt in a large saucepan and bring to a boil over medium-high heat. Reduce the heat to low, cover the pan and simmer until all the water has been absorbed and the rice is tender, 12 to 15 minutes. Mix in the lemon juice and cover and keep warm.

Heat the oil in a small nonstick saucepan over medium-high heat; add the mustard seeds, chili flakes, cinnamon and cloves. Cook, stirring about 1 minute.

Add the spice mixture to the rice and serve hot.

Spicy Eggplant Rice with Mint

Serves 6

1 cup dried coconut, unsweetened

8 dried red chili peppers, broken

1½ teaspoons coriander seeds

1 teaspoon cumin seeds

2 teaspoons sesame seeds

½ teaspoon green cardamom pods

½ teaspoon black peppercorns

¼ teaspoon ground turmeric

¼ teaspoon ground cloves

¼ teaspoon ground cinnamon

2 tablespoons vegetable oil

1 tablespoon mustard seeds

1 tablespoon fresh curry leaves, minced

1 pound eggplant, cut into 1-inch pieces

Salt to taste

1 tablespoon tomato paste

4 cups basmati rice, cooked

2 tablespoons mint leaves, chopped

In a medium pan, over medium heat dry-roast the coconut, chili peppers, coriander, cumin, sesame seeds, cardamom and peppercorns. Stirring until fragrant, about 2 minutes. Let it cool and grind in a spice or coffee grinder into a fine powder. Mix in the turmeric, cloves and cinnamon.

Heat the oil in a large saucepan over medium-high heat and add the mustard seeds; they should splutter upon contact with the hot oil. Quickly add the curry leaves, eggplant, salt and half of the ground spice mixture. Cover the pan and cook over medium-high heat the first 2 to 3 minutes, then reduce the heat to medium and cook until the eggplant is quite soft, about 10 minutes.

Add the tomato paste and cook about 2 minutes. Gently mix in the cooked rice, mint and the remaining ground spice mixture. Cover and cook over low heat, 5 to 7 minutes, to blend the flavors. Serve hot.

Brown Basmati with Caramelized Onions and Broccoli

Serves 6

1½ cups brown basmati rice, rinsed
and drained

2⅔ cups water

Salt to taste

4 tablespoons vegetable oil

6 cardamom pods

1 (1-inch) cinnamon stick

6 cloves, whole

4 small onions, thinly sliced

2 teaspoons sugar

1 teaspoon cumin seeds

1 teaspoon black mustard seeds

1 small head broccoli, cut into ½ -inch florets

1 teaspoon garam masala

In a saucepan over high heat, combine the rice and salt and bring to a boil. Reduce the heat to low, cover and simmer until all the water has been absorbed and the rice is tender, 12 to 15 minutes. Do not stir the rice, while it is cooking. Remove from the heat and rest about 5 minutes.

Heat 3 tablespoons of oil in a large nonstick saucepan over medium-high heat and cook the cardamom, cinnamon and cloves, stirring, about 30 seconds. Add the onions and cook, stirring as needed, until golden, about 5 minutes. Sprinkle the sugar over the onions, reduce the heat to medium low and continue to cook until they are dark brown. Using a slotted spatula, remove half the onions, drain them on paper towels and reserve for garnish.

In a small saucepan, heat the remaining 1 tablespoon of oil and add the cumin and mustard seeds; they should splutter upon contact with the hot oil, lower the heat and cover the pan until the spluttering subsides. Quickly add the broccoli and garam masala and stir for about 2 minutes. Transfer the rice to a serving platter and lightly mix in the broccoli.

Serve garnished with the reserved caramelized onions.

Stir-Fried Mushrooms and Red Chard Pilaf

Serves 6

2 cups water
1½ cups basmati rice, rinsed and drained
Salt to taste
1 teaspoon cumin seeds, roasted
3 tablespoons vegetable oil
1 pound white button mushrooms, cleaned and quartered
1 pound red chard, trimmed, washed and finely chopped
1 large clove fresh garlic, minced
2 fresh green chili peppers, minced
Salt to taste
1 tablespoon fresh cilantro leaves

In a medium saucepan, boil the water; add rice, salt and cumin seeds. Return to a boil. Reduce the heat to low, cover and simmer until the water is absorbed and the rice is tender, about 10 to 15 minutes. Transfer to a large bowl and keep warm.

In a large saucepan over medium-high heat, add 1 tablespoon of oil and the mushrooms until they release their juices, cooking until the mushrooms are golden, 5 to 7 minutes. Reserve in a bowl.

To the same pan, add the remaining oil and chard and cook, stirring, over medium-high heat until wilted, about 3 minutes. Add the garlic, green chili peppers and salt, reduce the heat to medium, cover the pan and cook until the leaves are soft, 7 to 10 minutes. Mix in the mushrooms.

Top the mushroom and chard mixture on rice and serve hot garnished with cilantro.

Cranberry Pilaf

Serves 6

2 tablespoons vegetable oil or clarified butter

2 (1-inch) cinnamon sticks

4 cardamom pods

½ teaspoon black peppercorns

1 large onion, thinly sliced

½ tablespoon ginger, minced

½ tablespoon garlic, minced

1 teaspoon saffron threads

1¼ cups basmati rice, soaked, rinsed and drained

2 cups dried cranberries

2⅓ cups water

¼ cup fresh cilantro, finely chopped

In a large nonstick saucepan, heat the oil over medium-high heat and cook the cinnamon, cardamom and peppercorns until fragrant, about 1 minute. Add the onion and cook stirring until golden, about 5 minutes.

Mix in the ginger, garlic and saffron, stir about 2 minutes. Then add the rice and cranberries (save a few for garnish) with the water and bring to a boil over high heat. Reduce the heat and simmer until all the water has been absorbed and the rice is done, 12 to 15 minutes.

Serve hot, garnished with cilantro and cranberries.

Layered Saffron Rice and Chicken Casserole

Serves 6

5 large cloves garlic, peeled

1 (3-inch) fresh ginger, peeled

1 tablespoon fresh mint leaves

2 fresh green chili peppers, stemmed

1 cup fresh cilantro, coarsely chopped

2 tablespoons fresh lime juice

2 cups nonfat plain yogurt, whisked until smooth

1 tablespoon garam masala

Salt to taste

2 pounds chicken, skinned and cut into serving pieces

4 cups water

1½ cups basmati rice, rinsed and drained

2 tablespoons vegetable oil or clarified butter

4 whole mace

6 cardamom pods

1 (1-inch) cinnamon stick

2 bay leaves

2 teaspoons cumin seeds

2 tablespoons fresh mint, chopped

2 tablespoons fresh cilantro, chopped

1 teaspoon saffron threads, soaked in ½ cup milk

1½ cups onions, sliced and crispy fried

2 tablespoons cashew nuts, toasted

Preheat the oven to 350°F.

In a food processor or a blender, add the garlic, ginger, mint, chili peppers, cilantro and lime juice to make a smooth purée. Transfer to a bowl and mix in the yogurt, garam masala and salt. Add the chicken and mix well, making sure all the pieces are well coated with the marinade. Cover and marinate at least for 8 hours or overnight in the refrigerator.

In a large nonstick saucepan, bring the water to a boil over high heat, add the rice. Once boiled, reduce the heat to medium low and cook, uncovered, until the rice is cooked half way, about 7 to 10 minutes. Drain the rice and discard the water.

Heat the oil over medium-high heat in a large nonstick, oven-safe saucepan, with a tight fitting lid.

Add the mace, cardamom, cinnamon, bay leaves and cumin seeds, stirring constantly until fragrant, about 1 minute.

Add the marinated chicken, all the marinade and sauté stirring frequently until lightly brown, about 5 to 10 minutes. Remove from the heat.

Add cilantro and mint on top of the chicken, then cover everything well with the partially cooked rice. Top the rice with the saffron milk, seal the pan well with aluminum foil and place the lid over the foil.

Bake in the oven for about 30 minutes. Remove from the oven, fluff the top of the rice lightly with a fork and add the onions and toasted cashews on top and serve.

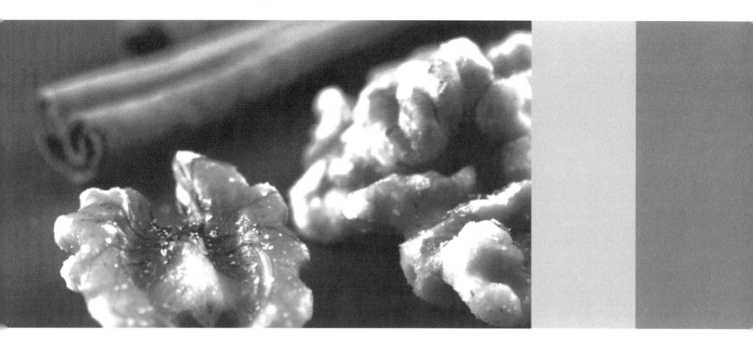

Wild Rice Pilaf with Walnuts

Serves 6

1½ cups water

⅓ cup wild rice, rinsed and drained

2 tablespoons vegetable oil

1 teaspoon cumin seeds

2 (1-inch) cinnamon sticks

4 cardamom pods

2 cloves garlic, crushed

2 bay leaves

2 green chilies, minced

1 cup basmati rice, soaked, rinsed and drained

2 cups water

Salt to taste

½ cup walnuts, toasted

1 tablespoon sesame seeds, roasted

1 tablespoon scallions, chopped

In a medium saucepan over high heat, add 1½ cups of water and the wild rice and bring to a boil. Reduce the heat to medium low, cover the pan and simmer until the all the water is absorbed and the rice is soft, about 30 to 40 minutes.

Heat the oil in a large saucepan over medium-high heat and add the cumin seeds, cinnamon, cardamom, garlic, bay leaves and chilies and cook, stirring, about 1 minute.

Add the cooked wild rice, the basmati rice, water and salt and bring to a boil over high heat. Reduce the heat, cover the pan and simmer until the rice is done, 10 to 15 minutes.

Serve hot, garnished with the toasted walnuts, sesame seeds and scallions.

Poultry

Spicy Bombay Chili Eggs
with Broccolini

Masala Scrambled Eggs with
Crumbled Paneer

Lemon Sage Chicken Tikka

Pan Roasted Onion Chicken

Lemon Pepper Chicken with Mint

Stir Fried Chicken with Cumin
and Peppers

Baked Mint Chicken

Duck Vindaloo

Cardamom Chicken

Green Chili Roast Chicken in
Banana Leaves

Grilled Chicken with Kokum
Apple Compote

Spicy Bombay Chili Eggs with Broccolini

Serves 6

6 large eggs
½ teaspoon ground cumin
Salt to taste
Freshly ground black pepper to taste
2 tablespoons vegetable oil
3 fresh green chilies, minced
6 scallions, minced
1 teaspoon ginger, minced
8 ounces broccolini, chopped
1 large tomato, chopped
1 teaspoon turmeric
2 tablespoons fresh cilantro, chopped

In a large bowl, beat the eggs with the cumin, salt and pepper.

In a large nonstick skillet, add oil over medium heat and cook the chilies, scallions, ginger and broccolini until soft, about 5 minutes, stirring constantly.

Add the tomato and turmeric and cook for 2 minutes.

Add the eggs and cook on medium heat until firm but not dry, about 3 minutes, stirring constantly. Once they have congealed, transfer them to a serving platter. Serve hot garnished with cilantro.

Masala Scrambled Eggs with Crumbled Paneer

Serves 6

2 tablespoons vegetable oil

1 small onion, chopped

1 large tomato, chopped

2 fresh green chilies, minced

1 tablespoon ginger, minced

1 tablespoon fresh lemon juice

Salt to taste

6 large eggs, lightly beaten

1 cup paneer cheese, coarsely crumbled

1 tablespoon fresh cilantro, chopped

Heat the oil in a large nonstick saucepan over medium-high heat and cook the onion, tomato and chilies, stirring, until most of the tomato juice evaporates, about 5 minutes.

Mix in ginger, lemon juice and salt. Stir.

Add the eggs and cook over medium heat, stirring constantly, until firm, about 2 minutes.

Mix in the cheese and cilantro and serve hot.

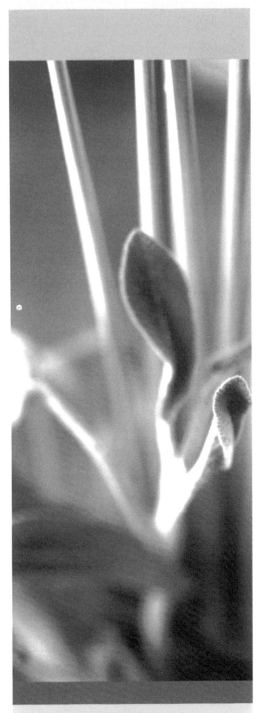

Lemon Sage Chicken Tikka

Serves 6

1 teaspoon cumin seeds, toasted
1 teaspoon coriander seeds, toasted
2 cups plain yogurt
4 cloves garlic , chopped
2 tablespoons ginger, chopped
3 tablespoons vegetable oil
2 tablespoons fresh lemon juice
1 teaspoon grated lemon zest
2 tablespoons fresh sage, chopped
Salt to taste
½ teaspoon turmeric
1 teaspoon garam masala
Freshly ground black pepper to taste
1 teaspoon chili powder
5 pounds skinless boneless chicken breasts, cut into
1-inch cubes
20 (12-inch) wooden skewers
6 lemon wedges for garnish

In a blender purée all ingredients except chicken until smooth.

Place the chicken in a large bowl and add yogurt mixture, stirring to coat the marinade all over the chicken. Cover and refrigerate for 4 to 6 hours.

Soak skewers in water for 30 minutes. While skewers are soaking, bring chicken to room temperature.

Preheat broiler to 375°F.

Brush a broiler pan lightly with oil. Divide chicken among skewers (5 cubes per skewer), leaving a ⅛-inch space between cubes and arrange the skewers in the pan. Broil chicken about 4 inches from heat, turning over once, until browned in spots and just cooked through, 10 to 12 minutes total and serve hot, garnished with lemon wedges.

Pan Roasted Onion Chicken

Serves 6

2 tablespoons vegetable oil

1 teaspoon cumin seeds

1 large onions, diced

1 teaspoon garam masala

2 pounds chicken, skinned and cut into
1-inch pieces

10 fresh curry leaves

2 (1-inch) cinnamon sticks

2 cardamom pods

1 tablespoon ground coriander

1 teaspoon ground cumin

Salt to taste

1 cup onions, sliced thinly and crispy fried

Heat the oil in a large nonstick saucepan over medium-high heat. Add the cumin seeds, onion and garam masala, cook until brown, about 5 minutes.

Add the chicken, curry leaves, cinnamon, cardamom, coriander, cumin and salt. Increase the heat and pan roast it until brown, about 5 minutes turning constantly. Reduce the heat to medium low and simmer covered until the chicken is tender, about 5 to 7 minutes. Add water if needed.

Serve hot garnished with fried onions.

Stir Fried Chicken with Cumin and Peppers

Lemon Pepper Chicken with Mint

Serves 6

1 tablespoon ginger, minced

1 tablespoon garlic, minced

3 tablespoons vegetable oil

Salt to taste

1 tablespoon coarsely ground black pepper

3 tablespoons lemon juice

1 tablespoon fresh grated lemon zest

1 cup fresh mint leaves, finely chopped

1 fresh green chili pepper, minced

1 teaspoon ground turmeric

1 large onion, thinly sliced

6 (4-ounce) chicken breasts, trimmed

In a medium bowl, mix in the ginger, garlic, 1 tablespoon of oil, salt, pepper, lemon juice, lemon zest, ½ cup mint, green chili and turmeric.

Add the chicken to the marinade and mix well. Cover and refrigerate for 2 to 3 hours.

Heat the remaining oil in a large nonstick skillet over medium-high heat and cook the onion, stirring until golden, about 5 minutes. Add the chicken and cook until brown, about 3 minutes on each side.

Reduce the heat and continue to cook, covered until the chicken is tender, about 5 to 7 minutes.

Serve garnished with remaining mint.

Stir Fried Chicken with Cumin and Peppers

Serves 4

1 pound boneless skinless chicken thighs, cut into 1-inch pieces

1 tablespoon ginger, minced

1 tablespoon garlic, minced

1 tablespoon cumin seeds, roasted and ground

2 tablespoons malt vinegar

1 teaspoon coarsely ground black pepper

Salt to taste

2 tablespoons vegetable oil

1 teaspoon cumin seeds

½ cup plain yogurt, whisked until smooth

1 large onion, diced

1 large red bell pepper, diced

Place the chicken in a large bowl. Add the ginger, garlic, cumin, vinegar, black pepper and salt and mix, making sure all the pieces are well-covered with the marinade. Cover with plastic wrap and marinate in the refrigerator for 4 to 6 hours.

Heat the oil in a medium, nonstick skillet and add the cumin seeds, they should sizzle upon contact with the hot oil. Quickly add the chicken with all the marinade and cook, turning as needed, until lightly golden on all sides, about 5 minutes.

Add the yogurt, stirring constantly to prevent it from curdling, then mix in the onion and bell pepper, and cook until all the juices evaporate and the chicken is rich golden in color and tender, about 10 to 15 minutes.

Baked Mint Chicken

Serves 6

1 tablespoon ginger, minced

1 tablespoon garlic, minced

2 tablespoons dried mint leaves

2 cups plain yogurt, whisked until smooth

2 teaspoons garam masala

Salt to taste

2 pounds chicken breasts and thighs, cut into 2-inch pieces

3 tablespoons canola oil

1 large onion, finely chopped

2 fresh green chilies, minced

2 tablespoons fresh mint leaves, minced

In a small bowl, mix together the ginger, garlic, dried mint, 1 cup yogurt, garam masala and salt. Add the chicken and mix well, making sure all the chicken pieces are well-coated with the marinade. Cover with plastic wrap and marinate in the refrigerator for at least 4 to 6 hours.

Preheat the oven to 350°F.

Heat the oil in an ovenproof saucepan with a tight fitting lid, over medium heat and cook the onion, stirring until brown, about 7 minutes. Add the chilies and stir for 1 minute.

Add the remaining yogurt, a little at a time, stirring constantly to prevent it from curdling and cook until it comes to a boil.

Mix in the chicken, plus the marinade. Cook, stirring for about 5 minutes. Remove from the heat and cover with the lid.

Place the pan on the oven and bake about 20 minutes, until the chicken is tender.

Serve hot garnished with mint leaves.

Duck Vindaloo

Serves 6

5 dried red chilies, crushed

1 teaspoon black peppercorns

1 teaspoon cumin seeds

1 teaspoon black mustard seeds

1 tablespoon ginger, minced

1 tablespoon garlic, minced

½ teaspoon sugar

Salt to taste

¼ cup white vinegar

2 pounds duck breasts, skinned and cut into 1-inch pieces

3 tablespoons vegetable oil

1 large onion, minced

¼ cup dry red wine

In a blender, add the chilies, peppercorns, cumin, mustard, ginger, garlic, sugar, salt and vinegar and blend it into a paste.

Add the spice paste to the bowl with the duck and mix to coat the meat. Cover and refrigerate for 4 to 6 hours.

Heat the oil in a wide heavy skillet over medium heat. Add the onion and sauté until tender and lightly browned, about 5 minutes.

Add the duck pieces (reserve any excess marinade) and sauté until the duck is browned on all sides. Add the reserved marinade and the wine.

Bring to a boil, then cover and lower the heat, simmer for 10 to 12 minutes until the duck is tender and cooked.

Cardamom Chicken

Serves 6

3 pounds chicken, cut into (2-inch) pieces
20 cardamom pods, seeded and ground
1 tablespoon ginger, minced
1 tablespoon garlic, minced
2 cups plain yogurt
2 teaspoons ground black pepper
2 teaspoons grated lemon zest
2 tablespoons clarified butter
2 cups coconut milk
6 green chilies, slit in half
2 tablespoons cilantro leaves, chopped
Salt to taste
3 tablespoons lemon juice

In a large bowl, place the chicken, cardamom, ginger, garlic, yogurt, pepper and lemon zest. Mix well until the chicken pieces are well coated. Cover and marinate for 4 to 6 hours.

Heat the clarified butter in a heavy-bottomed frying pan over medium-high heat. Add the chicken and cook until brown on both sides for about 5 minutes. Add the coconut milk to the pan, bring to a boil then add the chilies and the cilantro leaves. Simmer for 10 to 12 minutes or until the chicken is cooked. Season with salt and stir in the lemon juice.

Green Chili Roast Chicken in Banana Leaves

Serves 6

3 tablespoons lemon juice

Salt to taste

1 (4-pound) whole chicken

1 tablespoon oil

2 large onions, roughly chopped

1 tablespoon ginger, minced

1 tablespoon garlic, minced

5 green chilies, minced

3 tablespoons almonds, ground

1 teaspoon paprika

1 teaspoon turmeric

2 teaspoons garam masala

3 cups fresh cilantro, chopped

3 to 4 tender banana leaves

Rub the lemon juice and salt all over the chicken.

Heat the oil in a heavy-bottomed frying pan over medium heat, add the onion and cook until the they start to brown. Add the ginger, garlic and green chilies and cook for 2 minutes, or until soft. Add the almonds, paprika, turmeric and garam masala. Cook, stirring frequently for an additional minute. Allow the onion mixture to cool completely.

Place the cooled mixture in a food processor along with the cilantro, grind to a smooth paste. Rub the paste thoroughly all over the chicken and inside the cavity. Cover and refrigerate for 6 to 8 hours.

Preheat the oven to 400°F.

Soften the banana leaves by dipping them into hot water. Wipe the pieces dry as they become pliant. Tie the legs of the chicken together to keep them in place.

Wrap the chicken in the banana leaves, making sure that it is well covered. Tie a piece of kitchen string around the chicken like a package. Place the chicken in a roasting pan and bake for 1 hour, until the chicken is cooked and tender.

Unwrap the banana leaves from around the top of the chicken, baste the chicken with some of the juices and return it to the oven for 10 minutes until brown.

Grilled Chicken with Kokum Apple Compote

Grilled Chicken with Kokum Apple Compote

Serves 4

2 tablespoons coriander seeds

2 teaspoons cumin seeds

1 teaspoon cardamom pods

1 (1-inch) piece cinnamon stick

1 medium onion, roughly chopped

1 tablespoon ginger, chopped

½ teaspoon ground cloves

1 teaspoon cayenne pepper

4 tablespoons vegetable oil

Juice of 1 lemon

Salt to taste

1 pound (4 breasts) trimmed boneless chicken breasts

Place a small frying pan over low heat and dry-roast the coriander, cumin, cardamom and cinnamon until aromatic. Grind the roasted spices to a fine powder using a spice grinder.

Place onion, ginger, cloves, cayenne pepper, oil, lemon juice and salt in a blender or food processor until smooth. Add the roasted spice mixture to the onion paste.

Rub the chicken with the spice paste. Cover and marinate for 2 to 4 hours.

Preheat the grill to 350° F. Grill the chicken for 5 minutes on each side, or until the chicken is tender and cooked.

Compote

2 tablespoons butter

2 Granny Smith apples, peeled, cored and chopped

½ cup apple cider

1 teaspoon coriander seeds, roasted and ground

1 teaspoon cumin seeds, roasted and ground

2 tablespoons kokum, seeded and chopped

Cook the butter in small saucepan over high heat until golden brown. Add the apples and cook stirring until caramelized, about 5 minutes. Add the apple cider and cook until the liquid had evaporated, about 5 to 7 minutes. Mix in the coriander, cumin and kokum and cook for 1 minute. Set aside until ready to use.

Meat

Spice Grilled Lamb Chops with
Curried Couscous

Almond Crusted Leg of Lamb

Roasted Rack of Lamb with
Mint Crust

Lamb Chops with Rosemary and Lime

Honey Roasted Boneless Leg of Lamb

East Indian Chili with Red Beans

Kashmiri Lamb
Meatball Paprikash

Spicy Goan Beef Curry

Cashew Coconut Meatballs

Coorgi Pork Curry

Chipotle Pork Tikka

Aromatic Lamb with Green Peas
and Cumin

Classic Marinated Lamb Curry

Pan Roasted Lamb with Turnips

Cumin Coriander Beef Patties

Goan Meat Tarts

Spice Grilled Lamb Chops with Curried Couscous

Spice Grilled Lamb Chops with Curried Couscous

Serves 4

1 cup plain yogurt

1 tablespoon garam masala

Salt to taste

1½ pound (½-inch-thick) lamb chops

¼ teaspoon curry powder

¼ teaspoon ground turmeric

⅛ teaspoon ground cinnamon

1 teaspoon paprika

1½ cups water

2 tablespoons butter

1½ cups couscous

Mix together yogurt, garam masala and salt. Marinate the lamb chops with the yogurt mixture overnight or for at least 4 hours.

In a small heavy saucepan over medium heat, toast curry powder, turmeric, cinnamon and paprika, stirring constantly until fragrant, about 1 minute. Add water, salt and butter and bring to a boil. Place couscous in a heatproof bowl and pour in boiling water mixture, then quickly cover with a plastic wrap and let it stand for 5 to 10 minutes.

Preheat the grill or a broiler to 375° F.

Grill the lamb chops, turning over once for about 3 to 5 minutes on each side and set aside.

Fluff couscous with a fork and transfer it onto a serving platter. Place the lamb chops over the couscous and serve hot.

Almond Crusted Leg of Lamb

Serves 6

3½ pounds leg of lamb, trimmed of all visible fat

1 teaspoon ground cardamom

1 small onion, chopped

4 cloves garlic, minced

1 (1-inch) piece ginger, minced

3 green chilies, minced

2 teaspoons ground cumin

½ teaspoon ground cloves

1 tablespoon lemon juice

2 cups sour cream

½ cup blanched almonds, chopped

1 tablespoon brown sugar

½ cup plain yogurt

Pierce the leg of lamb with a sharp skewer all over so that the marinade will penetrate.

In a large bowl, mix together the cardamom, onion, garlic, ginger, chilies, cumin, cloves, lemon juice and 1 cup sour cream. Reserve.

Coat the lamb all over, using half the marinade. Cover with plastic wrap and marinate in the fridge for at least 6 to 8 hours. Cover the remaining marinade and refrigerate it.

Preheat the oven to 375°F.

Mix the reserved marinade with the ground almonds, brown sugar, yogurt and the remaining sour cream.

Crust the lamb all over with the almond mixture. Transfer the lamb to a shallow roasting pan and cover loosely with oiled aluminum foil and bake for 1 hour. Remove the foil and bake for another 30 minutes, until the lamb is cooked and the coating is browned.

To check if the lamb is cooked, insert a thermometer into the meat nearest to the bone reads 150°F for well done.

Serve whole and carve the meat at the table.

Roasted Rack of Lamb with Mint Crust

Serves 4

2 racks of lamb, about 1 pound each, trimmed if visible fat

2 tablespoons fresh lemon juice

1 tablespoon ginger, minced

1 tablespoon garlic, minced

1 teaspoon garam masala

Salt to taste

1 slice whole wheat bread, lightly toasted

1 tablespoon chopped cilantro

2 tablespoons ground dried mint leaves

1 teaspoon cumin seeds

2 tablespoons vegetable oil

1 tablespoon Dijon mustard

4 mint sprigs for garnish

Preheat the oven to 450°F.

In a large bowl, marinate the lamb with the lemon juice, ginger, garlic, garam masala and salt. Mix well, making sure all the pieces are well coated.

Place the bread in a blender or food processor and pulse until it forms coarse crumbs. Add the cilantro, mint and cumin, pulse to blend.

Heat the oil in a large ovenproof frying pan over medium-high heat. Add the lamb to the pan and cook, turning as needed, until browned on both sides, about 5 minutes. Remove the pan from the heat and brush the mustard over the rounded top and the front side of the racks. Gently pat the bread crumb mixture into the mustard.

Roast in the oven until a thermometer inserted into the meat reads 140°F for medium rare, 20 to 25 minutes. Transfer to a platter and let it rest.

To serve, cut the lamb between the ribs into separate bone-in chops garnished with the mint sprigs.

Lamb Chops with Rosemary and Lime

Serves 6

1 tablespoon black peppercorns

1 teaspoon cloves, whole

7 cardamom pods

1 tablespoon ground coriander

1 teaspoon ground cumin

½ teaspoon ground cinnamon

¼ teaspoon ground nutmeg

1 cup sour cream

1 tablespoon ginger, minced

1 tablespoon garlic, minced

Salt to taste

½ cup finely chopped fresh rosemary

2 tablespoons lime juice

2 tablespoons vegetable oil

2 pounds lamb chops, bone trimmed
of visible fat

1 cup water

2 sprigs rosemary

Lime wedges for garnish

In a spice grinder, grind together the peppercorns, cloves and cardamom.

In a small nonstick skillet over medium heat, roast the ground spices, coriander, cumin, cinnamon and nutmeg constantly stirring the pan, over medium heat until the spices are fragrant, about 2 minutes.

In a large bowl, mix together the roasted spices, sour cream, ginger, garlic, salt, rosemary, lime juice and oil. Add the lamb chops to the mixture and mix well, making sure all the pieces are well-coated with the marinade. Cover with plastic wrap and marinate in the refrigerator at least 4 to 6 hours.

Remove the lamb chops and reserve the marinade. Heat the oil in a large nonstick skillet over medium-high heat, cook the lamb chops turning once until golden brown, about 5 minutes on each side.

Mix water to the reserved marinade and add it to the skillet. Cover and cook over medium heat until the chops are tender and the sauce is thick, about 10 to 15 minutes.

Serve hot garnished with rosemary and lime.

Honey Roasted Boneless Leg of Lamb

Serves 6

1 pound fresh spinach, chopped

½ pound button mushrooms, chopped

1 cup almonds, chopped

¼ cup cranberries, dried

1 cup fresh cilantro, chopped

1 tablespoon garam masala

3½ pound leg of lamb, trimmed of visible fat, de-boned and butterflied

¼ cup malt vinegar

2 tablespoons vegetable oil

Salt to taste

1 teaspoon dark chili powder

1 cup sour cream

1 medium onion, minced

1 tablespoon garlic, minced

2 tablespoons melted honey, plus extra for drizzle

1 teaspoon clarified butter

1 tablespoon ground coriander

1 teaspoon ground cumin

½ teaspoon cayenne pepper

Mix together the spinach, mushrooms, almonds, cranberries, cilantro and garam masala.

Make 2-inch-long deep cuts, each about 2 inches apart, over the entire outside surface of the leg of lamb.

In a bowl, mix together the vinegar, oil, salt and chili powder and rub well over both sides of the meat, making sure you work it into all the cut sections. Spread the spinach mixture on the entire inside surface. Then roll the lamb into a log. Tie the roll with a kitchen twine crosswise and lengthwise to secure it.

Mix together the sour cream, onion, garlic, honey, clarified butter, coriander, cumin and cayenne pepper and rub well over the outside surface of the meat.

Cover with plastic wrap and marinate in the refrigerator for 6 to 8 hours.

Preheat the oven to 400°F.

Transfer the lamb to an ovenproof dish, along with its marinade and roast for 30 to 40 minutes.

Reduce the heat to 300°F and cook until the lamb is golden brown and tender, about 15 to 20 minutes.

Remove the string from the roast, cut the lamb into 1-inch slices and serve hot, drizzled with honey.

East Indian Chili with Red Beans

Serves 6

2 tablespoons vegetable oil

1 teaspoon cumin seeds

4 dried red chili peppers

1 teaspoon black mustard seeds

1 large onion, finely chopped

½ cup coconut, grated

1 tablespoon fresh ginger, minced

1 clove garlic, minced

2 tablespoons curry leaves, minced

1 tablespoon ground coriander

¼ teaspoon ground turmeric

1 teaspoon garam masala

Salt to taste

1 pound lean beef, ground

8 ounces canned kidney beans, rinsed and drained

1 medium tomato, chopped

1 cup water

1 cup coconut milk

½ cup fresh cilantro, chopped

Heat the oil in a large saucepan over medium-high heat, add the cumin, chilies and mustard seeds. They should splutter upon contact with the hot oil.

Add the onion and sauté, stirring constantly until softened, about 2 minutes, then mix in the coconut, ginger, garlic, curry leaves, coriander, turmeric, garam masala and salt. Stir until the mixture is golden, about 5 minutes.

Add the ground beef. Cook stirring until slightly brown, about 10 minutes.

Add the beans, tomato and water and bring to a boil over high heat. Reduce the heat to medium low and simmer until the sauce is thick, about 10 minutes. Add the coconut milk and half the cilantro and simmer for another 5 minutes. Serve hot garnished with cilantro.

Kashmiri Lamb Meatball Paprikash

Kashmiri Lamb Meatball Paprikash

Serves 4

2 pounds lean lamb, ground

1 (4-inch) peeled fresh ginger

1 tablespoon ground fennel seeds

1 teaspoon garam masala

1 teaspoon ground cumin

½ teaspoon ground cardamom

Salt to taste

2 tablespoons vegetable oil

1 (1-inch) cinnamon stick

1 teaspoon cumin seeds

1 large onion, chopped

1 tablespoon paprika

1 large tomato, diced

1 cup sour cream

½ cup water

1 tablespoon cilantro, chopped

In a food processor, add the lamb, ginger, fennel, garam masala, cumin, cardamom and salt. Grind the spice mixture until smooth.

Divide and shape the lamb into two ounce portions. Refrigerate until ready to use.

Heat the oil in a large saucepan over medium-high heat. Add the cinnamon, cumin seeds and onion. Cook the onion until golden brown, about 10 minutes. Add the paprika and fry for 30 seconds. Stir in the tomatoes, remove from heat and slowly stir in the sour cream.

Carefully add the chilled meatballs and bring to a boil. Simmer uncovered, for 30 to 40 minutes, over very low heat. Add ½ cup of water as necessary.

Cook until the meatballs are very tender and the sauce is thick. Serve garnished with cilantro.

Spicy Goan Beef Curry

Serves 6

7 dried red chili peppers

¼ cup malt vinegar

3 cloves garlic, peeled

1 (4-inch) ginger, peeled

1 large onion, chopped

1 tablespoon cumin seeds

3 teaspoons coriander seeds

2 teaspoons mustard seeds

1 teaspoon ground cinnamon

½ tablespoon soy sauce

½ teaspoon ground turmeric

2 pounds beef, cut into 1-inch pieces

3 tablespoons vegetable oil

5 curry leaves

3 tablespoons tomato paste

3 cups water

1 tablespoon cilantro, chopped

Soak the chili peppers in the vinegar for about 2 hours. In a food processor or a blender, grind together the chilies with the vinegar, garlic, ginger and onion until fine paste. Mix in the cumin, coriander, mustard, cinnamon, soy sauce and turmeric. Blend to make a smooth paste.

Add the spice paste to the beef and mix well in a large bowl, making sure all the pieces are well-coated with the marinade. Cover with plastic wrap and marinate in the refrigerator for at least 4 to 6 hours.

Heat the oil in a large nonstick saucepan over medium-high heat. Add the curry leaves and the beef with the marinade. Cook, stirring, over high heat until well-browned, about 5 to 7 minutes.

Add the tomato paste and water and cook until the beef is tender, about 30 to 40 minutes.

Serve hot garnished with cilantro.

Cashew Coconut Meatballs

Serves 4

1 pound beef, ground

½ cup cashew nuts

4 green chilies

1 teaspoon fennel seeds

1 small onion, minced

1 tablespoon garlic, chopped

1 cup coconut, grated

1 large egg

Salt to taste

2 tablespoons vegetable oil

1 medium onion, finely chopped

2 cloves garlic, minced

4 green chilies, minced

1 tablespoon ground coriander

1 tablespoon ground fennel

½ teaspoon ground cumin

1 teaspoon ground turmeric

2 medium tomatoes, chopped

Salt to taste

2 cups water

½ cup cilantro, chopped

In a food processor, add the beef, cashews, chilies, fennel seeds, onion, garlic, coconut, egg and salt and process until well-blended. Transfer to a bowl, cover and refrigerate for at least an hour.

Divide and shape the beef into two ounce portions. Refrigerate until ready to use.

Heat the oil in a wide heavy pot over medium-high heat. Add the onion and garlic and cook until softened, about 4 minutes, stirring occasionally to prevent sticking. Add the chilies, coriander, fennel, cumin and turmeric and stir. Add the tomatoes, salt and water and bring to a boil. Reduce the heat and simmer, uncovered for about 15 to 20 minutes.

Gently slide the meatballs into the sauce. Stir and move them around occasionally as they cook at a medium simmer of 20 minutes, or until cooked.

Serve hot garnished with cilantro.

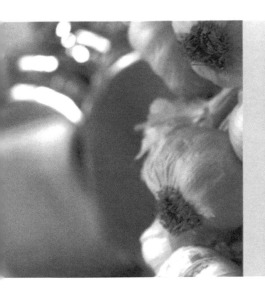

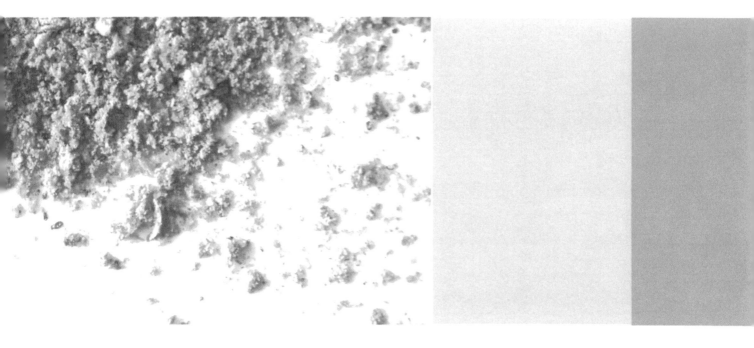

Coorgi Pork Curry

Serves 6

2 dried red chilies

1 tablespoon coriander seeds

1 tablespoon cumin seeds

2 teaspoons black mustard seeds

1 teaspoon black peppercorns

½ teaspoon turmeric

¼ teaspoon ground cinnamon

¼ teaspoon ground nutmeg

Salt to taste

2 tablespoons ginger, minced

3 cloves garlic, minced

1 fresh green chili, minced

½ cup coconut milk

2 tablespoons vegetable oil

1 large onion, finely chopped

1½ pounds pork, cut into 1-inch pieces

2 cups water

2 tablespoons cilantro, finely chopped

Place the red chilies, coriander, cumin, mustard seeds and peppercorns in a small skillet. Roast, stirring and shaking the pan, over medium heat until the seeds are a few shades darker, about 2 minutes. Grind in a spice grinder to make a fine powder. Mix in the turmeric, cinnamon, nutmeg and salt.

In the food processor or a blender, process the ginger, garlic, green chili and coconut milk until smooth. Mix in the roasted spice mixture and process again, adding up to ½ cup water, if necessary, to make a smooth paste.

Heat the oil in a large saucepan over medium heat and add the onions, sauté until brown, about 10 minutes. Add the spice paste and cook, stirring, until golden, about 10 minutes.

Add the pork and cook, stirring, until brown, about 15 minutes. Add the water and bring to a boil over high heat. Reduce the heat to medium low. Cover the pan and simmer until the pork is tender and the sauce is thick, about 30 minutes.

Serve hot, garnished with cilantro.

Chipotle Pork Tikka

Serves 4

1 medium onion, minced

3 cloves garlic , minced

2 tablespoons ginger, minced

½ tablespoon ground cumin

1 teaspoon ground coriander

4 teaspoons chipotle chili powder

Salt to taste

1 cup plain yogurt, whisked until smooth

1 pound pork tenderloin, cut into 1-inch cubes

3 tablespoons vegetable oil

3 bay leaves

1 large red onion, minced

1 clove garlic, minced

1 (1-inch) piece ginger, minced

2 dry chipotle chilies, crushed

½ cup fresh cilantro leaves, chopped

1 tablespoon garam masala

In a large bowl, mix the onion, garlic, ginger, cumin, coriander, chili powder, salt and yogurt. Add the pork to the marinade and mix well. Cover and marinate in the refrigerator for 2 to 4 hours.

Heat the oil in a heavy-bottomed frying pan, large enough to fit the pork in a single layer. Add the bay leaves, onion, garlic, ginger and chilies and stir for 4 minutes. Increase the heat to high and add the pork with the marinade. Stir constantly for 5 minutes, then reduce the heat to medium and let the meat and the juices simmer for 15 to 20 minutes. Cook until the pork is tender.

Serve hot, garnished with cilantro and garam masala.

Aromatic Lamb with Green Peas and Cumin

Serves 6

3 tablespoons oil

2 medium onions, chopped

1 teaspoon cumin seeds

2 tablespoons ginger, minced

4 cloves garlic, minced

4 green chilies, minced

2 bay leaves

1 pound ground lamb

2 tablespoons tomato paste

½ teaspoon ground turmeric

1 teaspoon chili powder

2 tablespoons ground coriander

2 tablespoons plain yogurt

Salt to taste

Freshly ground black pepper

½ cup water

1 cup frozen peas, thawed

¼ teaspoon garam masala

2 tablespoons ground cumin

5 tablespoons fresh cilantro, chopped

Heat the oil in a large saucepan over medium heat. Add the onion, cumin, ginger, garlic, chilies and bay leaves and fry for 3 to 4 minutes, until golden brown. Add the lamb and fry for 15 minutes, stirring occasionally to prevent from sticking.

Add the tomato paste, stir and lower the heat to a simmer.

Add the turmeric, chili powder and coriander and stir for 1 minute. Add the yogurt, salt and pepper and continue frying for 5 minutes. Add water and peas and simmer for 10 minutes until the lamb is cooked and tender.

Add the garam masala, cumin and chopped cilantro and stir for 1 minute before serving.

Classic Marinated Lamb Curry

Serves 6

3 medium onions, chopped

1 tablespoon chili powder

1 tablespoon ground cumin

¼ tablespoon turmeric

1½ cups plain yogurt

2 teaspoons garam masala

Salt to taste

2 pounds boneless leg of lamb,
cut into 1-inch cubes

3 tablespoons vegetable oil

5 cardamom pods

3 bay leaves

1 (1-inch) cinnamon stick

1 teaspoon cumin seeds

1 tablespoon ground coriander

4 fresh green chilies, minced

1 medium tomato, chopped

2 cups water

½ cup fresh cilantro, chopped

In a blender or a food processor, blend together onions, chili powder, cumin, turmeric, ½ cup yogurt, garam masala and salt.

In a large bowl, combine the yogurt onion mixture and lamb, making sure all the pieces are well-coated with the marinade. Cover with plastic wrap and marinate in the refrigerator, at least 4 to 6 hours.

Heat the oil in a large nonstick saucepan over medium-high heat, add the cardamom, bay leaves, cinnamon and cumin seeds. They should sizzle upon contact with the hot oil. Quickly add the coriander and then mix in the marinated lamb with the marinade and sauté over high heat, stirring, for 5 minutes. Reduce the heat to medium low, cover the pan and cook until most of the juices are dry, 15 to 20 minutes.

Add the green chilies, tomato, water and the remaining yogurt and bring to a boil over high heat. Reduce the heat to medium low, cover the pan and simmer until the lamb is tender and the sauce is thick.

Serve hot garnished with cilantro.

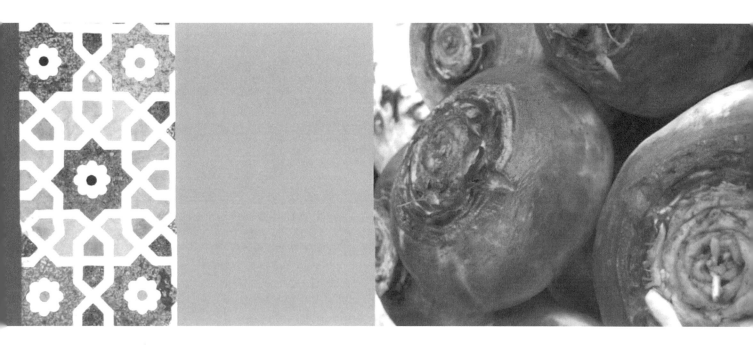

Pan Roasted Lamb with Turnips

Serves 6

2 medium onions, roughly chopped

4 cloves garlic, roughly chopped

2 tablespoons ginger, roughly chopped

2 green chilies

2 tablespoons vegetable oil

2 bay leaves

2 pounds boneless lamb, cut into 1-inch cubes

1 teaspoon chili powder

2 tablespoons ground coriander

2 tablespoons ground cumin

¼ teaspoon ground turmeric

½ teaspoon garam masala

1 tablespoon tomato paste

2 tablespoons plain yogurt

Salt to taste

Freshly ground black pepper

2 cups water

1 pound turnips, diced

Place the onions, garlic, ginger and chilies in a blender and process to a paste. Heat the oil in a large skillet on medium-high heat and add the onion mixture with the bay leaves. Cook, stirring until the onions turn golden brown, about 5 to 7 minutes. Add the lamb and stir until all the pieces are thoroughly coated with the onion mixture for 15 minutes.

Add the chili powder, coriander, cumin, turmeric and garam masala and stir in well. Cook for 1 to 2 minutes. Add the tomato paste and yogurt. Fry for another minute and season with salt and pepper. Pour in 2 cups of water a little at a time, stirring into the mixture after each addition, until you have a rich, thick sauce. Cover the pan and simmer for 30 minutes.

Add the turnips to the pan and continue simmering for another 20 to 25 minutes, or until both the lamb and turnips have completely softened and the oil has separated from the sauce and turned bright orange.

Cumin Coriander Beef Patties

Serves 4

1 pound lean ground beef

1 medium onion, finely chopped

1 teaspoon ginger, minced

1 teaspoon ground cumin

1 teaspoon ground coriander

½ teaspoon cayenne pepper

Salt to taste

¼ cup yogurt

1 teaspoon rice vinegar

¼ cup fresh cilantro, chopped

Place the beef in a bowl. Add the onion, ginger, cumin, coriander, cayenne pepper, salt, yogurt and vinegar and mix well with your hands or a rubber spatula, turning and mashing and kneading to blend the flavors and to get a smooth texture. Cover and refrigerate the mixture for at least an hour.

Mix in the cilantro. Shape eight medium patties: wet your hands with water, then scoop up about ¼ cup of the mixture. Use your hands to shape and press it into an oval or round ¾-inch thick. Give it several light but firm squeezes so it holds its shape, then place it on an oiled plate and repeat with the remaining beef.

To grill the patties, prepare a charcoal or gas grill to medium-high. Lightly oil the rack. Transfer the patties to the grill and cook, turning them after 5 to 6 minutes, until done.

Goan Meat Tarts

Makes 16 tarts

2½ cups all-purpose flour, plus extra for dusting

½ teaspoon salt

2 tablespoons sugar

¼ teaspoon baking powder

1 cup margarine, room temperature

1 large egg

3 tablespoons cold water

1 egg, whisked with 1 tablespoon water, for a wash

Make the pastry at least an hour before you wish to start baking.

Combine flour, salt, sugar and baking powder in a bowl and stir to mix well. Cut in the margarine until the mixture resembles coarse meal. Mix together the egg and water, pulling the dough together. If it is still crumbly, add an extra tablespoon of cold water and mix. When the dough just comes together, pull it into a mass. Cut it into two pieces (each will weigh just over ½ pound). Place each piece in a heavy-duty plastic bag, flatten out to a disk, seal well and refrigerate for at least 30 minutes.

Preheat the oven to 375°F.

Lightly dust your work surface with flour. Turn out the pastry from one bag, keeping the other refrigerated. Roll out to a 17 x 7-inch rectangle. Use a 3¼-inch round cookie cutter or glass to cut out 10 rounds. Place them on a baking sheet. Re-roll the scraps to make another 6 rounds. Place them on the sheet.

Lightly dust your work surface with flour again and repeat with the other piece of pastry, but set the rounds aside on your work surface.

Spoon 2 tablespoons of filling in the center of one of the circles on the baking sheet. Brush the edges with cold water, then place one of the reserved rounds on top. Pinch the edges together all around or press down with a fork to seal. Repeat with the remaining rounds. For a golden crust, brush with a little egg wash. Cut two slits in the top of each pastry.

Bake for 20 minutes or until golden. Set the pastries on a rack to cool for several minutes before serving or cool completely.

Beef Filling

4 dried red chilies, stemmed

½ teaspoon cumin seeds

2 cloves, whole

¼ teaspoon freshly grated nutmeg

¼ teaspoon mace

1 tablespoon vegetable oil

½ cup minced shallots

1 tablespoon ginger, minced

⅓ pound ground beef

Salt to taste

Freshly ground black pepper

1 tablespoon rice vinegar

1 teaspoon sugar

1 small tomato, finely chopped

Finely grind the chilies, cumin seeds and cloves in a spice or coffee grinder. Combine with the nutmeg and mace and set aside.

Heat the oil in a wide heavy skillet over medium heat. Add the shallots, ginger and spice mixture and cook for about 5 minutes, or until the shallots are softened. Add the beef and salt, stirring to break up any lumps. Add the pepper, vinegar and sugar and cook over medium heat, partially covered, stirring occasionally, until the beef has browned. Add the tomato and cook until the meat is thoroughly cooked, about 5 minutes.

Seafood

Grilled Sea Bass with Fenugreek
Chipotle Ketchup

Crispy Southern Indian Fried Fish

Roasted Red Snapper with Fresh
Green Chili Cilantro Pesto

Pan Braised Tilapia with Lemon
and Rosemary

Fish Wrapped in Banana Leaves

Curried Malabar Squid

Coriander Crusted Salmon with
Cilantro Cucumber Chutney

Konkan Chili Prawns

Goan Crab Cakes

Cumin Crusted Sea Scallops with
Mustard and Garam Masala

Tiger Prawn Curry with Lemongrass

Grilled Sea Bass with Fenugreek Chipotle Ketchup

Serves 6

2 tablespoons coconut milk
1 tablespoon ginger, minced
1 tablespoon garlic, minced
1 teaspoon red pepper flakes
3 tablespoons malt vinegar
2 teaspoons ground cumin
¼ teaspoon cloves, ground
½ teaspoon cinnamon powder
1 teaspoon ground paprika
Salt to taste
1 tablespoon vegetable oil
2 pounds sea bass fillets, about 1-inch thick, cut into 2-inch pieces
Lemon wedges for garnish

In a large bowl, mix together all the ingredients, except the fish and lemon wed

Add the fish and mix, making sure all the pieces are well-coated. Cover with pl
wrap and marinate in the refrigerator, at least for 4 hours.

Preheat the grill to medium high (375°F). Baste the grill or grill pan with oil to
prevent the fish from sticking.

Place the fish on the grill and cook, turning once or twice, until opaque and ju
flaky inside and lightly charred on the outside, 5 to 7 minutes. Serve hot with
lemon wedges and chipotle ketchup.

2 large tomatoes, diced
1 small onion, chopped
½ tablespoon garlic, minced
2 tablespoons tomato paste
1 tablespoon red wine vinegar
3 ounces chipotle chilies, minced
2 teaspoons ground cumin
Salt to taste
1 tablespoon fenugreek leaves, dried

In a small saucepan over medium-high heat, combine the tomatoes, onions,
garlic, tomato paste, vinegar, chilies, cumin, salt and fenugreek and bring it to
boil. Reduce the heat to medium and simmer, stirring until the liquid is redu
and thick, about 5 to 7 minutes. Cool before serving.

Crispy Southern Indian Fried Fish

Serves 6

2 pounds firm fish fillet, such as sole, halibut or pomfret, cut into 3-inch pieces

Salt to taste

1 tablespoon fresh lemon juice

⅓ cup rice flour

2 teaspoons cayenne pepper

1 teaspoon ground fennel

2 cups vegetable oil, for deep-frying

4 to 6 lemon wedges

Place the fish on a large platter. Sprinkle with salt and lemon juice and marinate about 30 minutes in the refrigerator.

Combine the rice flour, cayenne pepper and fennel in a flat pan.

With a paper towel, dry each piece of fish and then dredge in the rice flour mixture.

Heat the oil in a large nonstick skillet over medium-high heat until it reaches 350°F on a frying thermometer.

Deep-fry the fish until golden brown and crispy, about 4 to 5 minutes.

Transfer to a tray lined with paper towels to drain.

Serve hot garnished with lemon wedges.

Roasted Red Snapper with Fresh Green Chili Cilantro Pesto

Serves 6

1 whole red snapper, about 2 to 2 ½ pounds, cleaned and scaled

½ cup lime juice

½ teaspoon grated lime zest

2 tablespoons vegetable oil

Salt to taste

1 cup green chili cilantro pesto (recipe follows)

2 tablespoons fresh lime or lemon juice

Preheat the oven to 400°F. Score the skin of the fish in a diamond pattern.

In a shallow pan combine lime juice, lime zest, and 1 tablespoon of oil. Rub the fish all over with the lime mixture, then with salt.

Rub 1 cup of the pesto mixture into the slits and put the remainder in the fish's cavity. Lay the fish on the foil, pour on the remaining 1 tablespoon oil and spread it over the top of the fish.

Lightly coat a shallow baking dish with cooking spray. Wrap aluminum foil fairly tightly around the fish; use another piece of foil if necessary to ensure that the package is well sealed. Place it in a baking dish.

Bake for about 30 minutes; time will depend on the size and thickness of the fish. To test, peel back the foil a little and press on the flesh at the thickest part of the fish. It should yield a little and feel soft. The other test is to unwrap more of the fish and test the texture of the flesh: if it flakes with a fork, it is cooked.

Serve the fish warm on a platter, with extra pesto alongside as a condiment. Serve by lifting sections of the top fillet off the bone; when the first side is finished, flip the fish over to serve the second fillet. Drizzle excess pan juices on top of the fish.

Makes 1 cup

2 cups cilantro, chopped

6 green chilies, minced

1 tablespoon garlic, minced

2 teaspoons ginger, minced

2 tablespoons water

1 cup fresh or frozen coconut, grated

1 teaspoon cumin seeds, toasted and coarsely ground

3 tablespoons fresh lime juice

1 teaspoon sugar

Salt to taste

Place the cilantro, chilies, garlic, ginger and water in a food processor and process to a paste. Add the coconut and process to incorporate. Transfer to a bowl.

Add the coarsely ground cumin, lime juice, sugar and salt.

Serve or use immediately or refrigerate, covered, until ready to serve.

The pesto will keep for about 4 days in a well-sealed container in the refrigerator.

Pan Braised Tilapia with Lemon and Rosemary

Serves 6

6 (5-ounce) tilapia fillets

Salt to taste

1 teaspoon red chili powder

Juice of 1 lime

3 teaspoons vegetable oil

2 red onions, thinly sliced

½ cup red cherry tomatoes, halved

4 cloves garlic, minced

2 tablespoons ginger, minced

2 green chilies, minced

1½ cups vegetable stock

3 tablespoons malt vinegar

2 teaspoons grated lemon zest

1 sprig rosemary

Toss and season the tilapia fillets on both sides with salt, chili powder and lime juice.

In a large, nonstick frying pan, heat 2 teaspoons of oil over medium-high heat. Add the fish to the pan and sear on both sides until lightly browned, about 2 minutes on each side. Transfer to a plate and keep warm.

Add the remaining oil to the pan and add the onions, tomatoes, garlic, ginger and chili and sauté for 1 minute.

Stir in stock, vinegar, lemon zest and rosemary. Return the tilapia to the pan. Cover and simmer until the fish is opaque throughout. Test with the tip of the knife, 3 to 4 minutes.

Transfer the tilapia steaks to a serving platter. Spoon some sauce over each of the fish fillets.

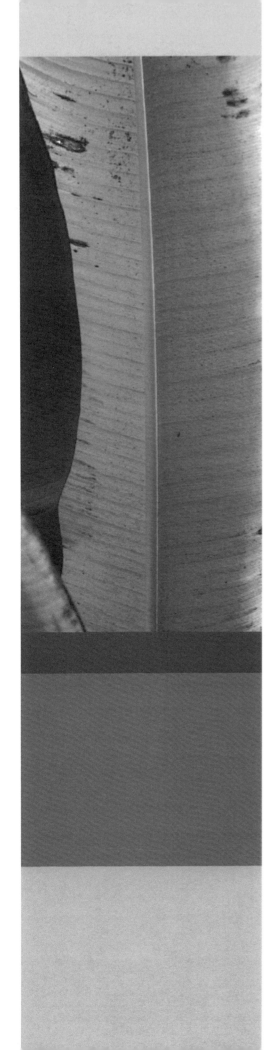

Fish Wrapped in Banana Leaves

Serves 4

1 pound fresh or frozen banana leaves cut into 10-inch squares
1 teaspoon cumin seeds, roasted
3 cups coconut, grated
4 green chilies, seeded and chopped
4 tablespoons cilantro leaves, chopped
1 tablespoon mint leaves, chopped
6 cloves garlic
1 green unripe mango, diced
3 tablespoons vegetable oil
Salt to taste
3 tablespoons lemon juice
1 pound fish fillet, sole, trout or pomfret, cut into 3- inch pieces
Mint leaves for garnish

Soften the banana leaves by dipping them into a saucepan of very hot water. Wipe the pieces dry as they become pliant. If you can't find banana leaves, use aluminum foil or parchment paper.

In a blender or a food processor, add the cumin, coconut, chilies, cilantro, mint, garlic and mango and grind to a smooth paste.

Heat 1 tablespoon of the vegetable oil in a frying pan and cook the paste over low heat until aromatic. Add salt and lemon juice.

Place the banana leaf squares on a work surface. Apply the paste liberally to both sides of each piece of fish. Place a piece of fish on each banana leaf and wrap up like a package, tying firmly with kitchen string.

In a large, heavy-bottomed frying pan which has a lid, heat remaining oil and shallow-fry the fish parcels together on one side. After 5 minutes, turn the packages over and fry for 5 more minutes. The leaves will darken and shrink. Cover the pan and cook the fish for a few more minutes.

You can also bake the fish package in an oven (450°F) for 20 minutes.

Fish packets can be assembled 2 hours ahead and chilled. Let stand at room temperature 20 minutes before cooking.

Open and serve each fish package on a plate. Garnish with mint leaves.

Curried Malabar Squid

Serves 6

1 teaspoon cumin seeds

1 teaspoon coriander seeds

1 teaspoon fennel seeds

2 teaspoons chili powder

1 teaspoon turmeric

2 pounds fresh squid, cleaned and cut into 1-inch rings

2 teaspoons soy sauce

1 tablespoon scallions, chopped

2 tablespoons oil

2 onions, thinly sliced

10 curry leaves

4 cloves garlic , crushed

2 tablespoons ginger, minced

½ cup coconut milk

3 tablespoons lime juice

Salt to taste

In a small frying pan over low heat, dry-roast the cumin, coriander and fennel until aromatic. Grind all three to a fine powder with the chili and turmeric, using a spice grinder. Toss the squid with the spice mixture, soy sauce and scallions.

In a heavy-bottomed frying pan, heat the oil over medium-high heat. Add the onions and sauté until lightly browned. Add the curry leaves, garlic, ginger and the marinated squid.

Sauté, stirring constantly for a minute.

Add the coconut milk. Bring to a boil. Simmer for 2 to 3 minutes, or until cooked and tender. Stir in the lime juice, season with salt and serve.

Coriander Crusted Salmon with Cilantro Cucumber Chutney

Serves 6

1 cucumber, peeled, halved lengthwise, seeded and thinly sliced
1½ cups cherry tomatoes, quartered
½ red bell pepper, seeded and cut into 1-inch slices
3 tablespoons red onion, chopped
2 tablespoons fresh cilantro, chopped
2 tablespoons fresh lime juice
3 teaspoons vegetable oil
2 teaspoons honey
1 teaspoon red pepper flakes
Salt to taste
6 salmon fillets, each 5 ounces and about 1-inch thick
Freshly ground black pepper to taste
3 tablespoons coriander seeds, toasted and coarsely ground
2 teaspoons garam masala
Lime wedges for garnish

In a bowl, combine the cucumber, tomatoes, bell pepper, onions and cilantro. Toss gently to mix. In a small bowl, whisk together the lime juice, 1 teaspoon of the oil, honey, red pepper flakes and salt.

Pour the lime juice mixture over the cucumber mixture and toss gently and set aside.

Sprinkle the salmon fillets on both sides with salt and pepper. Crust the salmon fillets on one side with the coriander seeds and garam masala. In a large, nonstick frying pan, heat the remaining 2 teaspoons of oil over medium-high heat. Add the fish to the pan crust side down, cook, turning once, until opaque throughout when tested with the tip of the knife, 4 to 5 minutes on each side.

Transfer to individual serving plates and top each with the cilantro cucumber chutney.

Serve hot garnished with lime wedges.

Konkan Chili Prawns

Serves 6

1 tablespoon vegetable oil

1 tablespoon ginger, chopped

3 cloves garlic, chopped

2 shallots, chopped

10 curry leaves

36 medium prawns, peeled and deveined

1 tablespoon soy sauce

2 tablespoons lemon juice

2 tablespoons cilantro, minced

2 tablespoons dry red chilies, chopped

¼ cup low fat yogurt, whipped until smooth

Salt to taste

2 tablespoons scallions, chopped

Heat the oil in a wok or very large sauté pan over high heat until very hot. Add the ginger, garlic, shallots and curry leaves and sauté for 1 minute.

Add the prawns and cook just until they start to turn pink, 2 to 3 minutes.

Add the soy sauce, lemon juice, chilies and cilantro and cook, stirring often, 2 to 3 minutes longer. Add yogurt and cook until the prawns are just cooked through.

Season with salt. Serve warm garnished with chopped scallions.

Goan Crab Cakes

Goan Crab Cakes

Serves 4

½ cup brown basmati rice, rinsed and drained

1½ cups water

Salt to taste

1 teaspoon vegetable oil

1 small red onion, chopped

1 clove garlic, minced

1 tablespoon ginger, minced

½ tablespoon green chilies, minced

7 ounces fresh lump crabmeat

1 tablespoon fish sauce

½ teaspoon chili sauce

2 tablespoons cilantro, chopped

1 egg, lightly beaten

3 tablespoons semolina

1 tablespoon vegetable oil

Fresh cilantro sprigs for garnish

In a saucepan, combine the rice, water and salt. Cover and bring to boil. Reduce the heat to low and cover. Simmer until the water is absorbed and the rice is tender, 45 to 50 minutes. Set aside.

In a small frying pan, heat the oil over medium heat, add the onions and sauté until translucent, about 5 minutes. Stir in the garlic, ginger and chilies and sauté until softened, about 1 minute.

In a large bowl, combine the crabmeat, onion mixture, fish sauce, chili sauce, cilantro and cooked rice. Toss gently with a fork to combine. Stir in the egg and mix until well-blended.

Sprinkle the semolina on a sheet of baking paper. Divide the crab mixture into 4 portions and form each portion into a 3½-inch patty. Dredge each patty in the semolina.

In a large frying pan, heat the canola oil over medium-high heat. Add the patties to the pan and fry, turning once and until golden brown on both sides, about 5 minutes on each side. Top with cilantro and serve hot.

Cumin Crusted Sea Scallops with Mustard and Garam Masala

Serves 4

3 tablespoons chili powder

3 tablespoons toasted cumin, ground

1 teaspoon salt

1 teaspoon freshly ground black pepper

¼ cup olive oil

1 teaspoon mustard seeds

2 cardamom pods

1 star anise

12 large sea scallops, rinsed and patted dry

Combine chili, cumin, salt and pepper in a medium shallow bowl. Dredge one side of each scallop in the spice mixture. Heat the oil in a large nonstick saucepan over high heat. Add mustard seeds, cardamom and star anise. Place the scallops in the heated pan, spice side down and cook for 20 seconds. Reduce the heat to low, turn the scallops and cook for 2 to 3 minutes more. Remove from pan and arrange the scallops around the platter. Drizzle the spice oil drippings from the pan over the scallops and serve.

Tiger Prawn Curry with Lemongrass

Serves 6

1 large red onion, sliced

½ cup vegetable oil

2 cloves garlic, minced

1 (1-inch) peeled ginger, minced

3 green chilies, minced

¼ cup chopped fresh lemongrass, tough outer leaves removed

2 tablespoons ground coriander

1 teaspoon ground cumin

1 teaspoon turmeric

Salt to taste

1 teaspoon freshly ground black pepper

½ teaspoon ground cinnamon

½ teaspoon ground cloves

1 (14-ounce) can unsweetened coconut milk

2 pounds jumbo tiger prawns or jumbo shrimp (about 24), shelled and deveined

In a large saucepan, cook onions in oil over medium-high heat, stirring occasionally, until slightly brown. Add garlic, ginger, chilies, lemongrass and remaining ingredients except coconut milk and prawns or shrimp; and cook over medium heat, stirring occasionally, about 5 to 7 minutes.

Mix in coconut milk and bring the sauce to a boil, stirring. Add prawns or shrimp and simmer, uncovered, stirring occasionally, until just cooked through, 3 to 5 minutes.

Serve hot.

Breads

Rosemary Naan

Griddle Fried Spicy Spinach Breads

Toasted Cumin Chapatis
with Orange

Fried Puffed Bread with Mint

Semolina Crêpes

Potato and Dill Stuffed Parathas

Spinach and Thyme Roti

Rosemary Naan

Serves 4

4 cups all-purpose flour
1¼ cups milk, warm
1 package (about 0.6 ounces) dry yeast
2 teaspoons nigella seeds
½ teaspoon baking powder
½ teaspoon salt
¼ cup rosemary, minced
1 egg, whisked
2 tablespoons vegetable oil
¾ cup plain yogurt

In a large bowl, sift the flour and make a well in the center. Add the yeast, nigella seeds, baking powder, salt and rosemary. In another bowl, mix the egg, oil and yogurt. Pour into the flour with 1 cup of milk to the flour and mix to form a soft dough. If the dough seems dry, add the remaining ¼ cup of milk. Turn onto a floured work surface and knead for 5 minutes or until smooth and elastic. Put in a oiled bowl, cover and leave in a warm place to double in size, about 2 to 3 hours.

Preheat the oven to 400°F.

Punch down the dough, knead it briefly and divide into 10 portions. Roll out the dough into 6 to 7-inch diameter circle. Arrange the rolled breads on a greased baking sheet. Bake on the top shelf for 7 minutes, turn over the naan and cook for another 5 minutes.

Serve hot.

Griddle Fried Spicy Spinach Breads

Serves 4

1½ cups whole wheat flour

2 scallions, minced

¼ cup cilantro, chopped

1 tablespoon ginger, minced

2 green chilies, minced

½ teaspoon salt

¼ teaspoon red pepper flakes

1 cup spinach, cooked and cooled

½ cup clarified butter

Place the first 7 ingredients in a medium bowl and mix well with your clean fingers. Add the spinach and enough water and mix until it starts to gather into a soft dough. Add 1 or 2 tablespoons more flour, if the dough seems sticky, or some water if it seems too firm.

Knead for about a minute, pressing your knuckles lightly into the dough, spreading the dough outward, then gathering the ends together toward the center with your fingers. Cover with plastic wrap or the lid of the bowl and set aside at least 1 and up to 4 hours.

Heat a griddle pan over medium heat. Divide the dough into 8 equal potions. Working with one portion at a time and keeping the rest covered, on a lightly floured surface, roll out each portion to for a 6-inch diameter circle.

Remove the excess surface flour prior to cooking. Place each rolled bread on the griddle, leave it to brown, about 7 to 10 seconds. Turn it over to brown on the other side. About 12 to 15 seconds. Turn over and smear the hot bread with clarified butter. Serve hot.

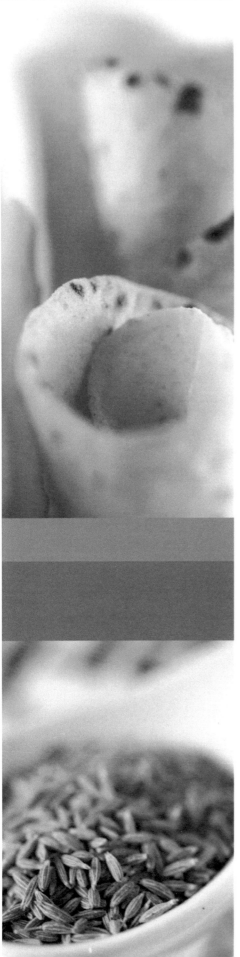

Toasted Cumin Chapatis with Orange

Serves 4

2 cups whole wheat flour
½ teaspoon salt
2 teaspoons cumin seeds, roasted
Zest of 1 orange
1 cup water
½ cup clarified butter

Sift the whole wheat flour, salt, cumin and orange zest into a bowl. Make a well in the center. Add water, enough to mix to form soft dough. Turn the dough onto a floured work surface and knead for 5 minutes. Place in an oiled bowl. Cover and rest for 30 minutes.

Heat a griddle pan over medium heat. Divide the dough into 8 equal potions. Working with one portion at a time and keeping the rest covered, on a lightly floured surface roll out each portion to for a 6-inch diameter circle.

Remove the excess surface flour prior to cooking. Place each rolled bread on the griddle, leave it to brown, about 7 to 10 seconds. Turn it over to brown on the other side, about 12 to 15 seconds. Turn over and smear with clarified butter.

Serve hot.

Fried Puffed Bread with Mint

Serves 4

1 cup whole wheat flour

½ cup all-purpose flour

¼ teaspoon cumin seeds, coarsely ground

¼ teaspoon salt

10 fresh mint leaves, minced

3 tablespoons vegetable oil

⅓ to ½ cup water

1 tablespoon dried mint leaves

Canola oil, for deep-frying

Prepare the dough in a food processor or by hand, mixing together all the dry ingredients and the fresh mint leaves, then adding the oil to blend, followed by ⅓ cup of water, until a dough is formed. Add more water if needed. Turn the dough onto a floured work surface and knead for 5 minutes. Place in an oiled bowl. Cover and rest for 30 minutes.

Divide the dough into 8 equal portions. Apply oil on both sides of the dough balls and flatten each with rolling pin into round discs, about 3 to 4 inches in diameter.

Pour oil into a medium saucepan so it is one-third full for deep frying over medium-high heat. Deep-fry the bread, turning once to ensure it puffs up. Drain on paper towels.

Serve immediately.

Semolina Crêpes

Makes 12 to 15

1 cup medium grain semolina
½ cup rice flour
2 tablespoons all-purpose flour
½ cup buttermilk
1 to 1½ cups water, as needed
Salt to taste
½ cup cilantro, chopped
2 tablespoons grated coconut
2 fresh green chilies, minced
1 tablespoon curry leaves, minced
½ teaspoon cumin seeds
3 tablespoons clarified butter

In a medium bowl, mix together the semolina, rice flour, all-purpose flour, buttermilk, 1 cup of water and salt and set aside until the semolina absorbs all the water, about 30 minutes.

Mix in the remaining ingredients and whisk for a few seconds, adding enough of the remaining water to make a thin batter of pouring consistency. If the batter becomes too thin, mix in some more rice flour.

Heat a nonstick frying pan over medium heat. Lightly brush the surface of the pan with oil. Stir the batter and pour a ladleful into the middle of the pan and quickly spread it out with the back of the ladle to form a thin pancake. Drizzle a little clarified butter around the edge to crisp up the pancake.

Cook until small holes appear on the surface and the edges start to brown. Turn over and cook until brown. Serve hot.

Potato and Dill Stuffed Parathas

Makes 14 to 16 breads

4 cups all-purpose flour

1 teaspoon salt

4 tablespoons oil

1½ cups water

½ pound potatoes, boiled, peeled and mashed

¼ teaspoon mustard seeds

½ onion, chopped

1 green chili, minced

2 cups dill, chopped

½ cup clarified butter

Sift the flour and salt into a bowl and make a well in the center. Add 2 tablespoons of oil and water and mix into a soft, pliable dough. Turn out into a floured surface, knead for 5 minutes and then place in a oiled bowl. Cover and allow to rest for 30 minutes.

Heat the remaining oil in a saucepan over medium heat, add the mustard seeds and let them pop. Add the onion and fry for 1 minute. Stir in the chili and dill, cook for another 2 minutes. Add the potatoes and cook over low heat for 5 minutes. Season with salt and cool.

Divide the dough into 14 portions and roll each into a 6-inch circle. Spread 1 tablespoon of the potato filling evenly over one half of each circle of dough and fold into a semicircle. Rub oil on half the surface area, fold over into quarters. Roll out until double in size. Cover the parathas with a cloth.

Heat an oiled griddle over medium heat. Remove the excess flour on each piece of dough and cook for 2 to 3 minutes. Turn over and cook until slightly brown, lightly brushing with clarified butter.

Serve warm.

Spinach and Thyme Roti

Spinach and Thyme Roti

Makes 20

4 cups spinach leaves, cooked and chopped

1 pound all-purpose flour

1 teaspoon salt

½ cup thyme leaves, chopped

1 teaspoon oil

1 cup water

1 cup clarified butter

Squeeze out the extra water from the spinach. Sift the flour and salt into a bowl and make a well in the center. Add the spinach, thyme, oil and water and mix to form a soft dough. Turn out the dough onto a floured surface and knead for 5 minutes. Place in an oiled bowl and cover to rest for 30 minutes.

Divide the dough into 15 balls. On a lightly floured surface, evenly roll out each portion to a very thin 6-inch circle.

Heat a griddle over a medium-high heat, oil it lightly and cook the roti one at a time. Cook for 2 to 3 minutes on each side. The roti will turn brown around the edges. Brush lightly with clarified butter and serve warm.

Desserts

Carrot Halwa with
Pineapple Compote

Phirni Custard with Figs and Honey

Pure Almond Milk Fudge

Spiced Almond Cookies

Sweet Yogurt Sundae with Saffron
and Pistachios

Cardamom Brownies

'Nankhatai' Indian Short
Bread Cookie

Pistachio Kulfi with Saffron
Crème Anglaise

Valrhona Chocolate Burfi with
Toasted Coconut

Shahi Bread Pudding Bites

Chai Crème Brûlée

Angel Hair Payasam with
Golden Raisins

Chocolate Cake with Ginger
and Dates

Orange and Saffron Yogurt Loaf

Pink Peppercorn Chocolate Truffles

Black Tea and Cinnamon Truffles

Carrot Halwa with Pineapple Compote

Serves 6

4 tablespoons clarified butter

1 pound carrots, peeled and grated

7 cups whole milk

1 teaspoon saffron threads

1 (14-ounce) can sweetened condensed milk

1 teaspoon ground cardamom

1 tablespoon pistachios, halved and roasted

Edible gold leaves (optional)

Compote

1 pound pineapple, diced

2 tablespoons butter

2 tablespoons sugar

½ cup pineapple juice

2 vanilla beans, split and scraped

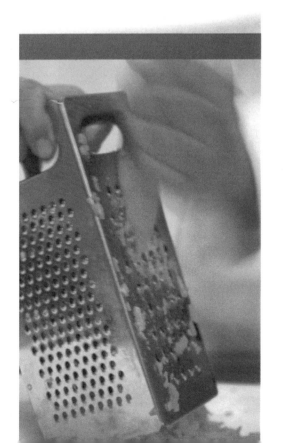

In a large saucepan, heat the clarified butter over medium-high heat. Add carrots and sauté for 5 minutes.

Add milk and saffron and cook, stirring over high heat until the milk comes to a boil. Reduce the heat to medium and continue to cook, stirring and scraping the sides of the pan often, until all the milk has absorbed into the carrots, about 30 to 35 minutes.

Mix in the condensed milk and cardamom and cook, stirring and scraping, until the mixture is quite dry, 10 to 12 minutes. Add the pistachios and continue cooking, stirring constantly, until it pulls away from the sides of the pan and is slightly golden, about 5 to 10 minutes.

Transfer to a serving dish and garnish with the edible gold leaves.

Serve hot or cold with pineapple compote.

To prepare the compote, sauté the pineapple with butter and sugar. Add the remaining ingredients and cook until soft and warm.

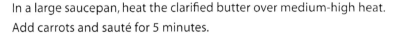

Phirni Custard with Figs and Honey

Serves 6

1 cup basmati rice, soaked, rinsed and drained

9 cups whole milk

1 teaspoon saffron threads

2 vanilla beans, split and scraped

¾ cup sugar

1 teaspoon ground cardamom

Figs and Honey Topping

10 ounces fresh or dried figs, halved

½ cup butter

1 tablespoon sugar

2 tablespoons honey

Place the rice in a blender along with 2 cups milk and blend for about 1 minute. The mixture will still appear grainy.

Place the remaining milk, saffron and vanilla in a large, heavy wok or saucepan and bring to a boil over high heat. Reduce the heat to medium and simmer, stirring and scraping constantly, until the milk has slightly thickened, about 5 to 7 minutes.

Add the blended rice to the simmering milk, stirring with a whisk constantly to prevent any lumps. Increase the heat to medium high and cook, until the custard is thick and creamy, about 5 minutes.

Add the sugar and cardamom, reduce the heat to low and cook for another 5 minutes to blend the flavors. Remove the vanilla beans and bring to room temperature (stir often to prevent a skin from forming) or covered with plastic wrap. Serve chilled with warm figs and honey mixture on top or on the side.

For the fig and honey compote, in a large saucepan, sauté figs with butter and sugar. Add honey and cook until figs are soft.

Pure Almond Milk Fudge

Makes 25 – 30 pieces

3½ cups almonds, blanched
2 teaspoons cardamom, ground
2 cups powdered milk
2 tablespoons clarified butter
¾ cup sugar
2 sheets edible gold leaf

Place a small frying pan over low heat and dry-roast the almonds until brown. Cool and chop in a food processor or with a knife. Line a 10 x 7-inch baking pan with waxed paper.

Combine the powdered milk and almonds in a large bowl and add the clarified butter, stir in the cardamom. Stir until well combined.

Combine the sugar and 1 cup of water in a heavy-bottomed saucepan and heat over low heat until the sugar melts. Bring to a boil and simmer for 5 to 7 minutes to make sugar syrup. Quickly stir the sugar syrup into the almond mixture, if you leave it too long it will stiffen. Spread the mixture into the baking pan (the mixture should be about ⅝-inch thick). Smooth with a greased spatula.

Place the gold leaf on top by inverting the sheets onto the surface and peeling off the paper backing. Allow to cool, then slice into diamond shapes. Serve cold.

Spiced Almond Cookies

Makes 20 cookies

½ cup unsalted butter, room temperature

1⅓ cups powdered sugar

2 teaspoons vanilla extract

1 teaspoon almond extract

¾ teaspoon ground allspice

¾ teaspoon ground cardamom

½ teaspoon ground cinnamon

¼ teaspoon salt

1 cup all-purpose flour

¾ cup finely chopped toasted almonds

Preheat oven to 350° F.

Using an electric mixer, beat butter, ⅓ cup of sugar, both extracts, spices and salt in medium bowl until creamy, about 3 minutes. Mix in flour and then stir in almonds. Do not over mix.

Using hands, roll dough into tablespoon-size balls. Place on a large baking sheet, spacing apart. Bake until pale golden, about 12 to 15 minutes. Cool on sheet for 5 minutes. Place remaining sugar in a large bowl. Working in batches, gently coat hot cookies in sugar. Cool cookies on rack.

Sweet Yogurt Sundae with Saffron and Pistachios

Serves 8

4 cups plain yogurt
1 teaspoon saffron strands
⅓ cup whole milk
1 teaspoon ground cardamom
¼ teaspoon freshly grated nutmeg
⅓ cup honey
¼ cup coarsely chopped pistachios

Line a large sieve or colander with cheesecloth. Wet the cloth with water, then place the sieve or colander over a bowl. Place the yogurt in the sieve to drain for 2 to 3 hours in the refrigerator. Discard the whey.

Turn the yogurt into a bowl and set aside.

 Lightly toast the saffron strands in a small dry skillet over medium heat, until brittle. Add the milk, cardamom and nutmeg, remove from the heat and stir in the honey until dissolved.

Whisk the mixture into the yogurt. Use a ladle to pour the yogurt into sundae cups or bowls. Top with a sprinkling of nuts and sauce.

Cardamom Brownies

Makes 20

5 ounces bittersweet chocolate, finely chopped

2¼ sticks (9 ounces) unsalted butter,
at room temperature

4 large eggs

1¼ cups sugar

15 cardamom pods, seeded and ground

1 cup all-purpose flour

1¼ cups pecans, lightly roasted
and coarsely chopped

Preheat the oven to 350ºF.

Butter a 9 x 12-inch baking pan, fit the bottom with a piece of baking paper and dust the inside of the pan with flour; tap the excess flour out and set aside.

Melt the chocolate in a bowl over simmering water or in a microwave oven. Remove the chocolate from the heat and cool slightly.

In a large mixing bowl, with a flexible rubber spatula beat the butter until smooth and creamy. Stir in the chocolate. Gradually add the eggs, then the sugar and cardamom, followed by the flour and nuts, stirring using a whisk until all the ingredients are incorporated. Do not beat or aerate.

Scrape the batter into the baking pan and smooth the top with a spatula. Bake for 20 to 25 minutes. The top of the cake will be dry, but a knife inserted in the center will come out wet. Transfer the pan on a cooling rack and allow the brownies to cool for 30 minutes.

Run a knife around the edges of the pan and unmold the brownies, remove the baking paper, cut the brownies and serve.

"Nankhatai" Indian Short Bread Cookies

Makes 20 cookies

2 cups all-purpose flour
Baking soda, a pinch
Salt, a pinch
1 stick (½ cup) unsalted butter, cut into cubes
¾ cup powdered sugar
¼ cup cashew nuts, roasted and ground
¼ teaspoon nutmeg
½ teaspoon cardamom
¼ teaspoon saffron
¼ cup clarified butter
Cashew halves for garnish

Preheat the oven to 350°F.

In a large bowl, sift the flour, baking soda and salt. Add the butter and cut into the flour using a spatula or a pastry blender until the mixture is sandy. Add the sugar, cashews, nutmeg, cinnamon, saffron clarified butter and knead it into smooth dough.

Do not over mix.

Place the dough in the refrigerator for 5 to10 minutes. Divide the dough into 20 portions. Roll into balls and arrange the rolled dough on a baking sheet lined with parchment paper, leaving about an inch of space between each one. Flatten each ball to form a fat disc, decorate with a cashew nut and bake for 10 to12 minutes until the sides of the cookies are beginning to brown.

Transfer the cookies to a rack to cool completely before serving.

Pistachio Kulfi with Saffron Crème Anglaise

Serves 6

5 cups whole milk

¼ cup sugar, or to taste

½ teaspoon ground green cardamom seeds

¼ cup pistachios, ground

¼ cup pistachios, coarsely chopped

Place the milk in a large saucepan and bring to a boil over high heat. Continue to boil, stirring, about 2 to 3 minutes. Reduce the heat to medium low and simmer, stirring and scraping the bottom and sides of the saucepan often, until the milk is reduced, about 45 minutes.

Mix in the sugar, cardamom seeds and ground pistachios. Cook, stirring, until the sugar melts and the pudding thickens again, about 5 to 7 minutes.

Transfer to kulfi molds or disposable 5 ounce plastic soufflé cups. Cover and place in the freezer until completely frozen, at least 4 hours.

To serve, dip each mold in hot water about 10 seconds, run a knife around the inside of the mold and transfer immediately to a dessert plate. Serve whole or cut into smaller pieces, drizzle with saffron crème anglaise (recipe follows) and chopped pistachios.

Saffron Crème Anglaise

Makes 4 cups

2½ cups milk

1 cup heavy cream

1 teaspoon vanilla extract

5 cardamom pods, crushed

2 teaspoons saffron strands

8 egg yolks

½ cup sugar

Place a medium bowl into a larger bowl filled with ice water. Place a fine mesh strainer inside the empty bowl. Set aside.

Combine the milk, cream, vanilla, cardamom and saffron in a medium-sized saucepan .Bring mixture just to a boil. Remove pan from the heat. Allow the mixture to stand for at least 30 minutes allowing the flavors to infuse into the milk. Strain and set aside.

In a medium bowl, beat the yolks and sugar together until the mixture has thickened and is a pale yellow color.

Bring the milk mixture just back to a boil.

Add approximately ½ cup of hot milk mixture to the egg mixture to temper the yolks, mixing while adding the hot milk. Then, while stirring constantly add the egg mixture back into the pan with the remaining milk and cream mixture.

Stir mixture constantly over medium-low heat until the mixture is the consistency of heavy cream or until you can draw a line with your finger along the back of the spoon and have the mixture leave a trail. Strain and cool over iced bowl. Store tightly covered for up to 2 days in the refrigerator.

Valrhona Chocolate Burfi with Toasted Coconut

Makes 36 pieces

1 cup sugar
½ cup water
1 pound almond paste, broken up into small pieces
1 cup clarified butter
1 cup Valrhona chocolate, melted
¼ cup almonds, ground
½ cup grated sweetened coconut, toasted
1 tablespoon powdered sugar, for dusting

In a heavy-bottomed, medium saucepan, combine the sugar and water and boil together until candy thermometer registers 225°F and a small amount of the syrup forms a thin thread between the thumb and forefinger when carefully sampled from the stirrer.

Reduce heat to medium and stir in the almond paste with ¼ cup of clarified butter. Stir in the rest of the butter in ¼ cup increments until all of it has been absorbed. Keep stirring over medium to medium-low heat. The mixture will become a single mass.

If the mixture begins to brown, lower the heat and continue stirring until the mixture becomes porous and starts to appear drier, about 10 minutes. Add the melted chocolate and mix.

Spread the mixture in a 9-inch-square baking pan and press into ½-inch thickness. Immediately sprinkle with the almonds and coconut, gently pressing them into the surface. While still warm, cut into 36 squares or diamond shapes. Dust with sugar and serve at room temperature.

Shahi Bread Pudding Bites

Serves 6–8

1 quart half-and-half

2 vanilla beans, slit in halves

1 teaspoon ground cardamom

¼ teaspoon ground nutmeg

¼ teaspoon ground cinnamon

½ cup sugar

1 (14-ounce) can condensed milk

3 cups vegetable oil, for deep-frying

18 slices thin white sandwich bread,
crusts removed and cut into triangles

½ cup pistachios, chopped

In a large saucepan, bring the half-and-half and the vanilla beans to a boil over medium-high heat. Reduce the heat to medium and simmer, stirring and scraping the sides often, until reduced to half, about 25 to 35 minutes.

Mix in the cardamom, nutmeg, cinnamon, sugar and condensed milk and remove from heat. Remove the vanilla beans.

Heat the oil in a large wok over medium-high heat to 300°F and fry the bread until golden, about 10 seconds. Transfer to paper towels to drain.

In a large flat-bottomed serving dish, arrange in a layer.

Spoon the thickened milk mixture over the bread which will absorb the sauce as it cools.

Serve chilled garnished with pistachios.

Chai Crème Brûlée

Serves 4

2 cups heavy cream
1 cup Assam tea leaves
1 vanilla bean, split lengthwise
4 cardamom pods
2 sticks cinnamon
1 teaspoon black peppercorns
1 teaspoon cloves, whole
4 egg yolks, lightly beaten
½ cup sugar
1 tablespoon unsalted butter, chilled and cut into small pieces

Place the cream, tea, vanilla bean, cardamom, cinnamon, peppercorns and cloves in a heavy saucepan and bring to a boil. Reduce the heat and simmer for 5 minutes, stirring occasionally. Set aside for 10 minutes to infuse and strain.

Whisk the egg yolks and 4 tablespoons of the sugar in the top of a double boiler over simmering water until pale and thick. Do not overcook.

Add the cream to the eggs in the double boiler, whisking constantly. Cook slowly, stirring occasionally, until the mixture thickens and coats the back of a spoon, approximately 10 to 12 minutes.

Remove from heat and whisk in the butter. Pour the custard mixture into a porcelain dish and chill thoroughly.

Just before serving, sprinkle the custard with remaining sugar and caramelize it with a kitchen torch. Fire quickly and evenly until the sugar is cooked but not burned.

Serve immediately.

Angel Hair Payasam with Golden Raisins

Serves 6

2 tablespoons clarified butter

1 cup angel hair pasta, broken into 1-inch pieces

4 cups whole milk

2 cups water

¾ cup sugar

½ cup condensed milk

½ cup golden raisins

½ cup cashew nuts, chopped

1 teaspoon ground cardamom

In a large frying pan, heat 1 tablespoon of clarified butter and pasta over medium heat until all pieces are lightly brown and give off a toasted aroma. Set aside.

In a medium saucepan, heat milk and water on medium high. As soon as the mixture boils, reduce heat to medium and add fried pasta. Continue to simmer for 6 minutes or until pasta is well cooked. Add sugar and simmer 15 minutes, stirring frequently to prevent sticking. When the mixture is done, it will have a creamy consistency. Add the condensed milk.

While the milk simmers in the saucepan with the pasta, fry the raisins and cashews with remaining clarified butter until lightly browned in the frying pan.

Add the raisins, nuts and cardamom to the milk. Stir and remove from the heat. Cover and chill for 3 to 4 hours.

Serve hot or cold.

Chocolate Cake with Ginger and Dates

Serves 8

8¾ ounces bittersweet chocolate, finely chopped
2¼ sticks unsalted butter, at room temperature
1 cup sugar
4 large eggs, at room temperature
½ cup plus 1 tablespoon all-purpose flour
2 teaspoons ginger powder
3 ounces moist dates, cut into small pieces

Preheat the oven to 350ºF.

Butter the inside of a 9-inch cake pan. Line the bottom with parchment paper, butter the paper and dust the inside of the pan with flour; tap out the excess and set the pan aside.

Place the chocolate in a bowl and melt it in a microwave oven. Set aside the chocolate to cool; it should feel just warm to the touch when mixing with the rest of the ingredients.

Put the butter and sugar in a mixing bowl fitted with the paddle attachment and beat on medium speed for about 5 minutes, scraping down the sides of the bowl frequently until the butter is creamy and the sugar well-blended. Add the eggs one at a time, beating for 1 minute after each addition. Reduce the mixer speed to low, pour in the cooled chocolate.

Add the flour, ginger and dates and mix into the batter.

Scrape the batter into the pan, smooth the top and slide the pan into the oven. Bake for 20 to 25 minutes or until the cake rises slightly, top may crack a bit and the cake may not entirely set in center. When you test the cake by inserting a slender knife into the center, the knife will come out slightly streaked with batter which is what you want. Transfer the cake to a rack to cool.

Once the cake is cool, chill it in the refrigerator for an hour or two to make it easy to unmold. Turn the cake out, remove the parchment and invert the cake onto a serving platter so that it is right side up. Allow the cake to come to room temperature before slicing and serving.

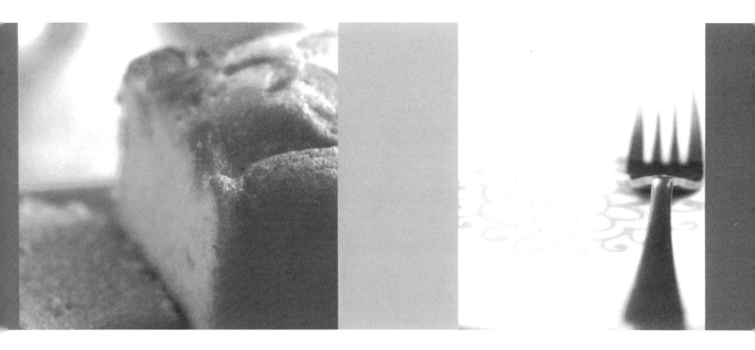

Orange and Saffron Yogurt Loaf

Makes 1 loaf

3 oranges

½ cup plus 2 tablespoons plain yogurt

1 cup plus 2 tablespoons sugar

2 teaspoons saffron strands

2 large eggs

½ cup vegetable oil

Finely grated zest of 1 lemon

Juice of 1 lemon

Finely grated zest of 1 orange

Juice of 1 orange

1 vanilla bean, split and scraped

1 cup plus 2 tablespoons all-purpose flour

2¼ teaspoons baking powder

Preheat the oven to 350ºF. Butter the inside of a 9 x 5 x 3-inch loaf pan.

Finely grate the zest of the oranges. Juice 1 of the oranges and reserve. In a large bowl, whisk together the yogurt, sugar, saffron and eggs. Add the vegetable oil, lemon zest, lemon juice, orange zest, orange juice and vanilla bean seeds. Add the flour and baking powder, whisking until just combined. Do not over mix.

Pour the batter into prepared pan. Bake until a knife inserted into the center of the cake comes out clean, 30 to 40 minutes. The cake will be dark golden on top and should pull away just a bit from the sides of the pan. If the crust begins to darken too much, cover the cake with a piece of aluminum foil. Cool in the pan on a wire rack for 10 minutes. Invert the cake onto the rack, remove the pan and cool completely.

Pink Peppercorn Chocolate Truffles

Pink Peppercorn Chocolate Truffles

Makes 40 truffles

9 ounces semisweet chocolate, finely chopped

1 cup heavy cream

2 tablespoons sichuan pepper, crushed

3½ tablespoons unsalted butter, softened

Cocoa powder, for dusting

Place the chopped chocolate in a medium bowl and set aside.

Using a small pot, bring the cream and pepper to boil. Remove from heat, infuse for 10 minutes. Strain the hot cream through a fine sieve over the chocolate. Add one-third of the pepper that is in the strainer back into the chocolate mixture and discard the rest. Allow the cream to soften the chocolate for 2 minutes. Using a whisk, stir the chocolate mixture slowly until smooth. Add the butter, stirring until melted. Transfer the chocolate cream mixture into a flat pan and cover with plastic wrap, making sure the plastic wrap touches the entire surface of the mixture. Refrigerate for at least 2 hours until the chocolate is set.

Place the cocoa powder in a shallow pan. Using a teaspoon dipped in hot water, form ½-inch balls of the chocolate mixture. If the mixture gets too soft while working, refrigerate until set. Roll the truffles in generous amounts of cocoa powder and store in an airtight container in a cool place for up to three weeks.

Black Tea and Cinnamon Truffles

Makes 5 dozen truffles

1 pound semisweet chocolate, finely chopped

2 cups heavy cream

1 cinnamon stick

½ cup tea leaves

4 tablespoons unsalted butter, softened

Cocoa powder, for dusting

Place the chopped chocolate in a medium bowl and set aside.

Using a small pot, bring the cream and cinnamon to boil. Remove from heat, add the tea and infuse for 5 minutes. Strain the hot cream through a fine sieve over the chocolate. Using the back of the spoon, press the tea leaves to extract as much flavor as possible. Allow the cream to soften the chocolate for 2 minutes. Using a whisk, stir the chocolate mixture slowly until smooth. Add the butter, stirring until melted. Transfer the chocolate cream mixture into a flat pan and cover with plastic wrap, making sure the plastic wrap touches the entire surface of the mixture. Refrigerate for at least 2 hours until the chocolate is set.

Place the cocoa powder in a shallow plate. Using a teaspoon dipped in hot water, form ½-inch balls of the chocolate mixture. If the mixture gets too soft while working, refrigerate until set. Roll the truffles in cocoa powder and store in an airtight container in a cool place for up to three weeks.

Drinks

Tangerine Carrot Cooler

Sparkling Ginger Lime Cooler

Ginger Cardamom Chai

Mango Yogurt Lassi with Saffron

Masala Mojito

Almond Date Shake

Watermelon Cranberry Sherbet

Salted Yogurt Lassi with Cumin

Cucumber Cooler with Mint

Pomegranate
Champagne Celebration

Spiced Hot Chocolate

Tangerine and Carrot Cooler

Tangerine Carrot Cooler

Serves 6

1 pound carrots, peeled and cut into dices
1 cup honey
¼ teaspoon fresh nutmeg, grated
½ gallon tangerine juice
10 to 12 ice cubes

In a blender, blend together all the ingredients. Pass the purée through a fine mesh sieve placed over a bowl. Serve chilled in a tall glass.

Sparkling Ginger Lime Cooler

Serves 2

1 (3-inch) piece peeled fresh ginger
½ cup coarsely chopped fresh mint leaves
½ cup fresh lime juice
6 cups sparkling water or club soda
½ cup sugar
1 teaspoon salt
¼ teaspoon ground black pepper
5 to 6 ice cubes

In a blender, blend together all the ingredients, except ice. Strain and serve over ice.

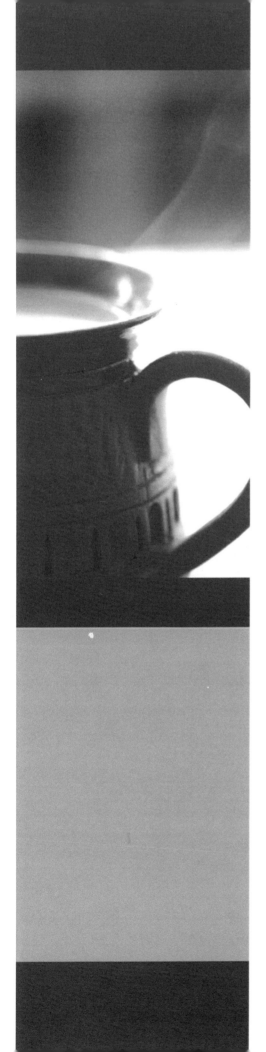

Ginger Cardamom Chai

Serves 4

2 cups water
¼ cup coarsely chopped fresh mint leaves
1 (1-inch) slice fresh ginger, crushed
4 cardamom pods, crushed
½ cup milk
2 teaspoons loose black tea leaves
Sugar to taste

In a medium saucepan, add the water, mint, ginger and cardamom and bring to a boil over high heat. Lower the heat to medium and continue to boil another minute to extract maximum flavor. Add the milk and bring to a boil once again. Add the tea leaves, turn off the heat, cover the pan and set aside to steep, about 3 minutes.

Pour through a strainer into teacups. Discard the spices and the leaves. Serve hot with the sugar.

Mango Yogurt Lassi with Saffron

Serves 4

4 cups vanilla yogurt
2 cups chopped ripe mango or canned mango pulp
1 cup crushed ice
2 tablespoons sugar
¼ teaspoon saffron strands, toasted and ground

Combine the ingredients in a blender until the yogurt is frothy. Serve cold.

Masala Mojito

Serves 6

½ cup honey

½ cup fresh lime juice

½ cup firmly packed fresh mint leaves

2 cups fresh grapefruit juice, chilled

2 cups fresh orange juice, chilled

2 teaspoons grated lime zest

1 teaspoon dry mango powder

1 teaspoon chat masala

1 lime, cut into 6 slices

In a small saucepan, combine the honey and lime juice, bring it to a boil over medium heat. Add the mint leaves and remove from the heat. Steep the honey mixture for 5 minutes. Pass the mixture through a fine mesh sieve placed over a bowl, pressing down on the leaves with the back of a wooden spoon. Refrigerate the syrup until cold.

In a large pitcher, combine the mint syrup, grapefruit juice, orange juice, lime zest, mango powder and chat masala.

Pour into tall, chilled glasses and garnish with lime slices.

Almond Date Shake

Serves 4

½ cup chopped pitted dates

2 tablespoons warm water

2 cups almond milk

1 teaspoon vanilla extract

2 ripe bananas

5 ice cubes

⅛ teaspoon fresh nutmeg, grated

Soak the dates with warm water for 5 minutes to soften, drain.

In a blender, combine the dates, almond milk, vanilla, bananas, ice cubes and nutmeg. Blend until smooth and frothy, about 40 seconds.

Pour into tall chilled glasses.

'Almond milk' is made from raw almonds that have been ground, soaked in milk and pressed.

Salted Yogurt Lassi with Cumin

Watermelon Cranberry Sherbet

Serves 6

2½ pounds seedless watermelon,
rind removed and diced

1 cup cranberry juice

¼ cup fresh lime juice

Sugar, to taste

1 orange, cut into slices

1 lime, cut into 6 slices

Place the melon in a blender or food processor. Process until smooth. Pass the purée through a fine mesh sieve placed over a bowl. Discard the pulp. Pour the juice into a large pitcher. Add the cranberry and lime juices and stir to combine. Add sugar to obtain desired sweetness. Refrigerate until very cold.

Pour into tall chilled glasses and garnish with fresh orange and lemon slices.

Salted Yogurt Lassi with Cumin

Serves 4

4 cups plain yogurt

2 cups water

1 cup crushed ice

3 teaspoon salt

¼ teaspoon toasted cumin, ground

1 tablespoon mint, chopped

¼ teaspoon cumin seeds, toasted

In a blender, add the yogurt, water, ice, salt, cumin and mint and blend until frothy. Strain and serve cold garnished with cumin seeds.

Cucumber Cooler with Mint

Serves 4

3 quarts water, chilled
3 English cucumbers, peeled and coarsely sliced
½ cup mint leaves
½ cup lime juice, fresh squeezed
¼ teaspoon roasted cumin, ground
¼ cup sugar

In a blender, add ½ cup of water with 1 cup of sliced cucumbers. Blend. Add more cucumbers and mint and blend. Continue until all the cucumbers are puréed.

Strain the cucumber juice of its seeds into a very large pitcher. Add the remaining water, lime juice, cumin and sugar.

Chill before serving.

Pomegranate Champagne Celebration

Serves 2

2 sugar cubes
2 fluid ounces pomegranate juice
6 fluid ounces dry champagne
4 teaspoons pomegranate seeds

Place one sugar cube in the bottom of each champagne flute. Pour half the pomegranate juice over it, then half the sparkling wine. Drop a few pomegranate seeds into each glass. Serve chilled.

Spiced Hot Chocolate

Serves 2

2 cups water

¼ cup brown sugar

4 ounces bittersweet chocolate

¼ cup cocoa powder

1 cinnamon stick

⅛ teaspoon ground nutmeg

1 hot red chili pepper, halved and seeded

Place the water and sugar in a medium saucepan, stirring until the sugar dissolves and bring it to a boil. Add the chocolate, cocoa powder, cinnamon, nutmeg and chili, stirring with a whisk and gently bring it to a simmer for 1 minute. Take off the heat and allow it to infuse for 10 minutes then strain to remove the chili and the cinnamon stick. Whip the hot chocolate in a blender.

Serve immediately in large cups or pour into a container to cool. Hot chocolate can be made up to 2 days ahead and kept tightly covered in the refrigerator.

To reheat the chilled chocolate, pour it into a medium saucepan, set the pan over low heat and bring it to a slow boil. Remove the pan from the heat, whip the chocolate for a minute in a blender.

Accompaniments

Garlic Chutney with Peanuts
and Tamarind

Wasabi and Green Chili Chutney

Pomegranate Mint Chutney

Coconut and Red Chili Sambal

Masala Hummus with Almonds

Plum Tomato Mustard Dip

Cranberry and Meyer
Lemon Confit

Potato Raita with Chives
and Cumin

Pan Roasted Eggplant Pachadi
with Sesame

Beet and Pineapple Raita

Mango and Roasted
Red Pepper Chutney

Pickled Green Papaya

Garlic Chutney with Peanuts and Tamarind

Makes 1 cup

½ cup peanuts, roasted
10 large cloves garlic, peeled
2 green chili peppers
1 cup fresh cilantro leaves
3 tablespoons tamarind paste
5 tablespoons water
1 teaspoon sugar
Salt to taste
1 tablespoon oil
1 teaspoon mustard seeds
5 curry leaves
1 teaspoon sesame seeds

In a food processor or a blender, blend together the peanuts, garlic, chilies and cilantro until minced. Add the tamarind paste, water, sugar and salt and mix again to make a smooth purée. Add more water if needed for blending. Adjust the seasonings.

Heat the oil in a large saucepan over medium-high heat and add the mustard seeds, lower the heat and cover the pan until the spluttering subsides. Add the curry leaves and sesame seeds and stir about 30 seconds. Add the tamarind mixture to the pan and simmer over low heat for 2 minutes. Cool and serve immediately or refrigerate up to two weeks.

Wasabi and Green Chili Chutney

Makes 1 cup

1 tablespoon wasabi paste

2 green chilies

5 scallions, coarsely chopped

1 cup fresh mint leaves, trimmed

3 cups fresh cilantro, coarsely chopped

4 tablespoons fresh lime juice

1 tablespoon low fat mayonnaise

2 teaspoons sugar

Salt to taste

In a food processor or blender, mix together the wasabi, green chilies and scallions until minced. Add the mint and cilantro and process, scraping the sides with a spatula, until puréed. As you blend, drizzle the lime juice through the feeder tube into the bowl and process until the chutney is smooth.

Add the mayonnaise, sugar and salt and blend. Transfer to a bowl and serve immediately or refrigerate up to two weeks.

Pomegranate Mint Chutney

Makes 1 cup

1 small red onion, coarsely chopped
2 green chilies, coarsely chopped
1 tablespoon fresh lemon juice
4 tablespoons water
4 cups fresh mint leaves
1 cup fresh cilantro, coarsely chopped
2 teaspoons dried pomegranate seeds, ground
1 teaspoon sugar
Salt to taste
2 tablespoons fresh pomegranate seeds for garnish

In a blender or a food processor, add the onion, chilies, lemon juice and 2 tablespoons of water and blend until smooth. Add the mint an cilantro blending until puréed. Add the remaining water, if needed.

Add the pomegranate seeds, sugar and salt and blend again. Adjust the seasonings. Transfer to a bowl and serve immediately or refrigerate up to two weeks. Garnish with fresh pomegranate seeds.

Coconut and Red Chili Sambal

Makes 2 cups

1 pound shredded coconut, fresh or frozen

3 dried red chilieses

1 tablespoon sambal chili paste

1 (2-inch) ginger, peeled

3 tablespoons fresh lemon juice

1 cup plain yogurt

1 cup fresh cilantro, coarsely chopped

Salt to taste

1 tablespoon vegetable oil

1 teaspoon black mustard seeds

2 tablespoons curry leaves, minced

In a food processor or a blender, blend together the coconut, chilies, sambal and ginger until minced.

Add the lemon juice, yogurt and cilantro and process, scraping the side of the bowl a few times with a spatula until as smooth as possible. Add the salt and transfer to a serving bowl.

Heat the oil in a small nonstick saucepan over medium-high heat and add the mustard seeds and curry leaves. Lower the heat and cover the pan until the spluttering subsides. Quickly add to the chutney and stir lightly as a garnish.

Serve immediately or refrigerate for up to two weeks.

Masala Hummus with Almonds

Makes 3 cups

1 cup almonds

2 cups canned garbanzo beans, rinsed and drained

2 tablespoons sesame seeds, roasted

5 cloves garlic, chopped

¼ cup fresh mint leaves

¼ cup fresh lemon juice

1 teaspoon sugar

Salt to taste

½ teaspoon ground black pepper

2 teaspoons cumin seeds, roasted and ground

1 teaspoon garam masala

In a food processor or a blender, blend together the almonds, garbanzo beans, sesame seeds and garlic until puréed with a little water to make a smooth paste. Add the mint, lemon juice, sugar, salt, pepper, cumin and garam masala and blend. Serve cold as a dipping sauce.

Plum Tomato Mustard Dip

Makes 1 cup

1 tablespoon coriander seeds

1 teaspoon cumin seeds

½ teaspoon black peppercorns

¼ cup vegetable oil

2 teaspoons black mustard seeds

2 teaspoons curry leaves, minced

3 whole dried red chili peppers

2 large cloves fresh garlic, minced

½ cup red onion, minced

1 teaspoon paprika

Salt to taste

2 large plum tomatoes, chopped

2 tablespoons tomato paste

2 tablespoons vinegar

¼ cup water

In a spice or a coffee grinder, grind together coriander, cumin seeds and peppercorns to make a fine powder.

Heat the oil in a small saucepan over medium heat and add the mustard seeds, curry leaves and chili peppers. Lower the heat and cover the pan until the spluttering subsides. Add the garlic and onion, stir a few seconds, then add the ground spices, paprika and salt and cook, stirring, another 2 minutes.

Add the chopped tomato, tomato paste, vinegar and water. Cover the pan, reduce the heat to low and cook, stirring occasionally, until the chutney is thick and fragrant. Reduce to about 1 cup, about 10 to 15 minutes. Serve hot or cold.

Cranberry and Meyer Lemon Confit

Cranberry and Meyer Lemon Confit

Makes 3 cups

1 tablespoon vegetable oil

1 cinnamon stick

2 star anise

3 cloves, whole

2 tablespoons fennel seeds

2 tablespoons peeled and minced fresh ginger

1 pound cranberries, fresh

Zest of 5 Meyer or regular lemons

Juice of 2 Meyer or regular lemons

2 cups sugar

6 cups water

Pinch of saffron threads

Salt to taste

3 tablespoons red wine vinegar

Heat the oil in a large saucepan over medium-high heat and cook the cinnamon, star anise, cloves, fennel seeds and ginger, stirring, about 30 seconds.

Add the cranberries, lemon zest, lemon juice, sugar, water, saffron and salt and bring to a boil over high heat. Simmer, stirring occasionally, until slightly thickened, about 15 to 20 minutes.

Reduce the heat to medium, add the vinegar and cook until the mixture is thick, about 10 minutes. Transfer to a bowl, let it cool and serve at room temperature, or refrigerate at least 2 hours and serve chilled. This can be stored in an airtight container in a refrigerator for up to 3 months.

Potato Raita with Chives and Cumin

Serves 4

1 large potato

2½ cups plain yogurt, whisked until smooth

2 teaspoons cumin seeds, toasted and ground

1 teaspoon black peppercorns, toasted and ground

Salt to taste

½ cup chives, minced

½ red bell pepper, finely chopped

Boil the potato in lightly salted water to cover until tender, then peel and chop into 1-inch dices.

Place the yogurt in a serving bowl, mix in the potato, salt and half the cumin and pepper. Add the chives and bell pepper. Serve garnished with the remaining cumin and pepper.

Pan Roasted Eggplant Pachadi with Sesame

Serves 4

1 tablespoon vegetable oil
1 teaspoon garlic, minced
1 small red onion, minced
1 small oval eggplant, cut into 1-inch pieces
3 cups plain yogurt, whisked until smooth
Salt to taste
1 teaspoon sesame oil
1 tablespoon sesame seeds, roasted

Place the vegetable oil in a large saucepan over medium-high heat and cook the garlic and onion, stirring until golden, about 1 minute. Add the eggplant and cook, stirring, until golden brown, 5 to 10 minutes. Cover the pan and cook over low heat until the eggplant pieces are very soft, 5 minutes. Let it cool.

Place the yogurt in a serving bowl. Add the salt, mix in the cooled eggplant with the pan drippings. Serve garnished with the sesame oil and sesame seeds.

Beet and Pineapple Raita

Serves 4

2 medium beets, whole

2 cups plain yogurt, whisked until smooth

1 cup sour cream, whisked

8 ounces pineapple, diced

5 scallions, minced

1 teaspoon garlic powder

1 green chili, minced

Salt to taste

½ teaspoon freshly ground black pepper

2 tablespoons cilantro, chopped

Place the beets in a small pan with water to cover by 2 inches and bring to a boil over high heat. Reduce the heat to medium low, cover the pan and simmer until tender, about 15 minutes. Remove from the heat, cool, peel and dice. Set aside to cool.

Mix the yogurt and the sour cream in a bowl and add the beets, pineapple, scallions, garlic, chilies, salt and black pepper. Garnish with the cilantro and serve.

Mango and Roasted Pepper Chutney

Mango and Roasted Red Pepper Chutney

Makes 3 cups

2 pounds mangoes, peeled and diced
½ cup white balsamic vinegar
¼ cup honey
¼ cup dried cherries
Salt to taste
2 tablespoons vegetable oil
1 medium onion, chopped
1 (1-inch) piece fresh ginger, minced
3 cloves garlic , minced
1 teaspoon ground cumin
1 teaspoon ground coriander
1 teaspoon chili powder
1 roasted red bell pepper, diced

Toss together mangoes, balsamic vinegar, honey, cherries and salt. Set aside.

In a medium saucepan over medium heat, add the oil and onions, sauté stirring occasionally, until cooked, about 5 to 7 minutes. Add ginger, garlic, cumin, coriander and chili powder. Reduce heat to low and cook, stirring for about 1 minute.

Stir in mango mixture and simmer, stirring occasionally, until mangoes are tender, about 15 to 20 minutes. Add the red pepper and cook for one minute. Serve cold.

Pickled Green Papaya

Makes 4 cups

4 red chilies, chopped
1 large red onion, chopped
1 (2-inch) piece ginger, minced
4 cloves garlic, minced
4 tablespoons black mustard seeds
2 cups vinegar
1 tablespoon mustard oil
1 cup brown sugar
Salt to taste
1 teaspoon ground turmeric
1 pound green papaya, peeled and diced

In a blender or a food processor, add the chilies, onion, ginger, garlic, mustard seeds and 1 cup of vinegar and blend to make a paste.

Heat the oil in a large saucepan over medium heat, cook the paste and remaining vinegar until fragrant and reduced. Add the sugar, salt, turmeric and papaya and simmer for 5 minutes.

Remove from the heat and cool before serving. This can be stored in an airtight container in a refrigerator for up to 3 months.

Acknowledgments

There are so many people to thank for their support and all their help to make this book possible:
Priyu, who gave me invaluable support, testing the recipes and believing in me. My parents in India for their support.

Praja, a talented, designer for her precision, focus and unique flair brought an innovative edge and visual perspective to this cookbook.

Vikas Khanna, who shared the passion, talent and knowledge to make this cookbook a reality. I am also grateful to so many friends and family members who inspire and are always there for me. There are friends and fellow chefs who share their passion for food.

Jack Turkel for creating beautiful photography. Kiran (KK), Atul Jain and Anil Rohira. My team and co-workers who help me everyday. Maya and Jay, my second family who opened their kitchen to me to test my recipes.

I also thank the following for their support. Rush Sherman, Niriti Nagpal, Steve Bain, Manny, Angela Lindo, Jerry Rieley, Naina, Kwaku and Bob.

Hari Nayak

Modern Indian Cooking is a collection of the efforts of so many people who came together to help us produce this great book; Hari Nayak, who pushed me to pursue it in the first place, came up with the wonderful ideas of recipes and worked days after days to develop these recipes.

My talented team and co-workers who have helped me develop some of the most creative recipes in Indian Cuisine.

My parents, who have supported my decision to get into the food world. My brother Nishant and my sister Radhika for being a part of my years that I spent learning my grandmother's recipe of cooking and serving food with love.

My beautiful nieces Ojasvi and Saumya who are my biggest fans. Karan Sandhu, Vitaly Kurbatsky and Susannah Monty, my dear friends who have encouraged me to develop more global flavors.

Vikas Khanna

Index

CPSIA information can be obtained
at www.ICGtesting.com
Printed in the USA
LVRC081457020821
694321LV00003B/42